Surviving the Toughest Race on Earth

Surviving the Toughest Race on Earth

MARTIN DUGARD

Photography by DiZinno

The McGraw-Hill Companies

New York · San Francisco · Washington, D.C. · Auckland · Bogotá
Caracas · Lisbon · London · Madrid · Mexico City · Milan · Montreal
New Delhi · San Juan · Singapore · Sydney · Tokyo · Toronto

International Marine/
Ragged Mountain Press
An Imprint of The **McGraw-Hill** Companies

2 4 6 8 10 DOC 9 7 5 3 1

Copyright © 1998 by Ragged Mountain Press.

Library of Congress Cataloging-in-Publication Data
Dugard, Martin.
Surviving the toughest race on earth / by Martin Dugard.
p.   cm.
ISBN 0-07-018129-2
1. Raid Gauloises (Adventure race)   2. Athletes—Biography.
3. Adventure and adventurers—Biography.   I. Title.
GV1038.2.R35D84   1998
796.6'3'092—dc21   97–32961
[B]   CIP

Design by Dennis Anderson, Duluth, MN
Production by Mary Ann Hensel and Dan Kirchoff

For Callie

Contents

Foreword

HERE, AT the end of the millennium, an extraordinary thing is happening in sports. There is a new kind of athlete, participating in a new kind of sport. This new athlete competes not for fame, or money, or career, but simply for adventure and for the experience of living—if only for the span of the event—at the very brink of human strength and endurance. For this, the athlete will travel literally to the ends of the earth, to places so desolate and so devoid of the comforts of modern life they might be from a distant time, or another planet.

What are these new athletes looking for?

They are trying to discover what they are capable of doing as men and women without the assistance of the modern world. They want to know extremity, because there is life in risk, and nobility in the breach.

They want to know nature, not the tame woods of the park, but nature raw, where exposure is not an accident, and where predators run free.

They are looking for all this and more, everything within their skills and fitness, as a sport and as a portal into this very beautiful and alien garden. And they want to share it with teammates and friends who embrace their vision of a life lived fully.

As a reporter, I have always loved to be involved in the events I write about. Participation provides a knowledge and sensibility of an event that cannot be achieved by mere observation. So I have found it inspiring to watch Martin Dugard pushing himself in the worst possible conditions as a journalist, and then sharing the pain and the joy of the competitors as a participating athlete. And I'm proud to have been able to play a part in the events that Martin reports, events that have sharpened in such fine athletes and competitors a sense of adventure and a passion for living.

GERARD FUSIL
Paris, January 1998

Surviving the Toughest Race on Earth

Lesotho, 1997

What I really want to do is quit, I think as I push my mountain bike
up yet another rutted South African trail on the eleventh day of the
Raid Gauloises. I've had enough of this foolishness—this suffering.
The temperature is 120 degrees. I've hiked, rafted, canoed, and climbed
over 350 miles. My feet resemble raw hamburger and I am chafed in
the most obscure places. I have definitely lived the promise that race
organizer Gerard Fusil made when I implored him to let me compete.
"You," he said, "will suffer."

I WANTED to do the Raid because it is the world's toughest endurance
race. Period. It's eight to twelve days of competition performed in a state
of constant peril. Tougher than the Ironman triathlon. Tougher than the
Tour de France. Tougher than the Iditarod sled dog race. Held in a different remote corner of the world each year, it seeks nothing less, in the
words of Fusil, than "to push individuals to their mental, physical, and
emotional limits."

It is a stage race with five-person teams, each team having at least
one woman, required to navigate hundreds of miles by land and by
water—and even, occasionally, by air. The first race, in 1989, featured
whitewater rafting and mountaineering in a course that led competitors
from one side of New Zealand to the other. The Madagascar Raid in
1993 included skydiving, rock climbing, and desert orienteering. There
was camel riding as part of Oman in 1992, dugout canoes in the 1990
Costa Rica event. Registered participants are told only the name of
the country and the disciplines to train for. Actual course location and
order of events aren't revealed until the prerace meeting two days
before competition begins.

The Raid has its roots in the childhood longing of Fusil, a man born 100 years too late. "I always dreamed," the fifty-year-old French journalist told me once, looking out across the Madagascan dawn, "of being an explorer." Buoyed by that dream, he designed a race that is the modern equivalent of colonial adventures past. Like Stanley and Livingstone, Byrd and Peary, and legions of other explorers, competitors race through primitive lands, unaided by motorized transport. The prize money is small. And, as when only the first explorer to reach a new land could claim its riches in the name of his king or queen, only the first-place Raid team receives the prize.

I had written about the Raid since 1992, when Americans first began competing. I'd attended three times. So I knew of its intangibles, how the misery of being cold and wet and tired breaks down teams until they quit in despair. And how even surefire winning teams fall short due to circumstance—things like an inability to locate water, or simple map reading errors that precipitate mind-boggling ramblings off course. Imagine a race in which you wander for twelve hours in the wrong direction, then have to retrace your steps to start all over again, and you get the picture.

Ironically—or perhaps fittingly, given the vast number of office-bound dreamers in this day and age—the Raid's competitive roster is loaded with individuals in rather innocuous occupations. Engineers, insurance agents, dentists, and biologists are more likely to compete than mountain climbers and rafting guides. This diversity gives the event an everyman feel. Red wine, even cigarettes, are evident in the days before competition. And while prerace conversations are invariably full of back-slapping and well wishes, the subtext is apprehension to the point of horror. "How will I face myself if I quit?" competitors seem to be thinking. "Do I really have what it takes to finish?" They turn to the Raid as if it were sonar, testing the depths of their character by plumbing, over the course of its sleepless days and nights, what they might never discern in a lifetime of Ironman triathlons. It is a never-discussed fact that fewer than one-third of the teams finish. "You can't think of quitting," points out Pat Harwood, the Navy SEAL commando who anchored Team American Pride in 1993 and 1994, "you just have to keep putting one foot in front of the other."

There is another quality to the Raid, an intangible called "The Spirit of the Raid." It is all-pervasive and all-encompassing, a quiet mystique that implies both a code of honesty among competitors and the unfailing belief that if it's possible for anything to go wrong, it will, in fact, go wrong. It's what drives competitors to go on when their feet are bloody and blistered, or to share their last drops of water with other teammates, even other teams. The Spirit of the Raid may be the real reason why teams ante up $15,000 apiece for the privilege of pushing themselves beyond mere endurance for a solid week or more, all the while threatened by leopards and leeches, rocks and rivers, rain and— caving's indoor equivalent—bat guano. It cannot be easily understood or explained, just felt. And as the Raid grows in popularity, the line to experience this ubiquitous sensation gets longer and longer, and every year, more and more teams are told they cannot enter. So I should consider myself lucky to be biking through the land of the Zulus, rubbed raw in all the wrong places.

A video crew in a dusty white Pathfinder pulls alongside. They are French, imperious, smoking. "I'm a journalist," I yell to the driver. "My team has quit. I have no maps, no food, and no emergency beacon. I want out of this race. Can you give me a ride to the finish line?"

Silence. And in that chasm, subtext: the rivalry between writers and video types. They view us as sanctimonious purists tied to the musty anachronism of the written word; we view them as techno-weenies with only a passing awareness of aesthetics. For me to invoke professional courtesy—privilege existing in concept but not reality—is an act of debasement. We both know it. Worse, I'm clinging to that awareness as a marker for my desperation.

He gives me the once-over and grabs something off the seat next to him. "You wanted to do the Raid," he says, thrusting two tins of sardines and a yellow circle of processed cheese out the window, "so do the Raid." And he speeds off. Feeling as if I've been kicked, I stuff the food in my backpack and swig a mouthful of muddy river water from a liter bottle. Then I pedal on, feeling the suffering just that much more acutely than a moment before.

PART I

Beginnings

CHAPTER 1

Leaving Normal

The history of adventure racing in America began February 21, 1991. It read like this:

QUEPOS, Costa Rica—A gentle rain began to fall soon after midnight, streaking the mud on my glasses and softening the sound of my horse's hoofs on the jungle floor. In the humid dark, the contralto voices of a million frogs thrummed, and the crazy blue flashes of a world of fireflies painted a brilliant canvas of motion and light....

THUS BEGAN a four-day, 10,000-word serialization in the *Los Angeles Times* by staff writer Jon Markman. He'd been invited by Gerard Fusil to compete as part of an all-journalist team in the 1990 Raid in Costa Rica. His tale was riveting. The first installment ran on a Sunday. I read it at my kitchen table, engrossed in every word, staring at the vibrant photographs of jungle and competitors. The next three parts I brought to work with me. Too enthralled to wait until lunch hour, I smuggled the paper into the men's room and hid in a stall to do my reading. Markman's story was too cool to be believed, a dramatic account of a race difficult beyond words.

Starting with a canoe paddle into the jungle from Limon, on Costa Rica's Caribbean side, thirty-three teams raced across the isthmus, concluding on the Pacific Ocean some eleven days later with a parachute jump into the resort of Quepos. Markman wrote of the tension of competing as part of a disparate team of individuals, with personality clashes par for the course; of slipping through mud for days on end; of intense heat and mosquitoes and snakes and jaguars; of conquering fears and emerging from the journey more in tune with himself and his environment; of racing his hardest, getting lost in the jungle, and never giving up the will to win, even when his team was dead last.

The words were evocative, like when he compared the jungles of Costa Rica with the Jungle Cruise at Disneyland. And poetic, as Markman finally bathed in the joy of finishing the unfinishable.

I knew nothing about canoeing or mountaineering or skydiving, but somewhere in my subconscious I felt a powerful sensation telling me not only that the Raid would be a stupendous adventure, but also that I was destined to compete. I know that sensation—the first time I met my wife I looked into her eyes and knew I was going to marry her. I trust that sensation. And as terrifying as Markman's piece was (Costa Rica being a country of crocodiles, impenetrable jungle, and scads of venomous snakes—so many that teams carried their own antivenin injections), the attraction was all the stronger for the danger.

Given my career at the time, it's no wonder I was quietly in search of adventure. I lived with a daily sense of dread that I would labor forever in my unfulfilling marketing job solely for the paycheck. Every moment of every day that I spent inside the major corporation I worked for was like doing time in a white-collar penal colony. And though I tried switching careers, firing off resumes to every conceivable type of corporation, from running shoe manufacturers to PR firms, there was either no response or the money was entry-level. I was, in a word, stuck—Papillon with a briefcase. The living, breathing embodiment of "corporate lackey."

It was my own doing. I took the job straight out of college, thinking that suits, ties, corporate hierarchy, and an office with a phone plus a personal computer were just about all a man could ask from life. And it is for some people. But not, I found, for me. This didn't make me feel superior to my coworkers, it made me envious. I desperately wanted what they seemed to have: a career for which they had a passion. That's the rub. I couldn't, and still can't, imagine getting up day after day to labor in a job I wasn't meant for, going to lunch when given permission, and having to account for every minute of my time, knowing that somewhere, some supervisor is keeping track. That's misery. Life's too short.

Funny thing was, I kept getting promoted. The more I wanted out, the higher I rose in the company. I started as a buyer of piping and electrical fixtures, but within three years was attending senior executive-level meetings as marketing coordinator/aide de camp for one of the company's vice-presidents. I wish I could say the promotions were the result of hard work or savvy, but it was really plain dumb luck. Searching for a job within the company where I wouldn't feel like a square peg in a round hole, I transferred laterally enough times that I eventually slipped through the cracks into a job of import. Things like that happen within the anonymity of multinational corporations.

My boss, whom I alternately worshipped and feared, was a white-haired, broad-shouldered Englishman. His adult life had been spent inside the corporate world, building oil refineries and highways from Baton Rouge to Beirut to New Delhi. Keith Thomson reveled in nuance: Machiavellian power plays, pointless meetings, the daily minefield of phone calls and strategy sessions into which productivity had to be sandwiched. There was nothing trivial or petty to Keith about the corporate world. It was the best, most respectable method of making a living a man could endeavor to pursue. His workday started very early and ended very late.

So mine did, too. And though I was without a doubt the worst employee in the history of corporate America, he was kind enough to predict a future for me. The mentoring process meant showing up at 5:30 most mornings and working into the night; rethinking the marketing budget or writing a speech, or merely sitting in yet another meeting with a bunch of guys in ties and suits with late-in-the-day rumples. Which would have been fine—hard work being good for the soul and all—if I'd felt marketing or the corporate world was my calling. But try as I might to convince myself that was the case, I couldn't. And as much as I enjoyed Keith's company and corporate insights, I was deathly afraid he would see through my facade into the impossible dream that ran around and around my brain, inspiring and tormenting me at once.

My dream was to quit, some way, somehow. I wanted to travel the world, visit adventure. Outside of honeymooning in the Canadian provinces of Alberta and British Columbia, where glacier-fed rivers ran clear, I'd never left the United States. My history minor in college had given me a craving to see battlefields, ruins, museums—all the stuff of great civilizations. I knew where pirates sailed and settlers died, and desperately wanted to see those places. My worst fear was that I would grow old and die never having seen the world firsthand, but only in books, forming opinions from images conjured by others.

I began pursuing the dream by doing freelance sportswriting. The few thousand dollars I made annually wasn't enough to allow me to strike out on my own, but fueled my imagination. The thought of becoming a full-time writer carried a romance that spirited me away during many a humdrum meeting. More than once I had to have a direct question repeated because I was gone. In the stratosphere. Daydreaming. Being my own man and living my own life. Nevertheless, a year and a half elapsed between Markman's Raid article and the life-changing phone call of November 10, 1992. It was late afternoon. The caller was British, somehow polite and brash at once. His name, he said before a single second of the conversation had elapsed, was Mark Burnett. On November 27 he was leading the first-ever American team to an obscure French race called the Raid Gauloises—had I heard of it?— through the Arabian Peninsula kingdom of Oman. The race would begin December 6. Sometime about eight days later, if all went well, Burnett's squad would show the French just how tough Americans really were. They would march across the final stretch of desert and cross the finish line in first place.

I was intrigued. It turned out Burnett had read a story of mine in *Runner's World* about a gruesome race held at a Marine Corps Air Station near my house. Called the Volkslauf, the 10-kilometer event mandated that all participants wear long pants and combat boots. The course consisted not just of running, but of a low crawl under barbed wire, a blast from a fire hose, several chest-high vaults, and a half-mile slog through a muddy drainage ditch. The mud was the worst. Even the Navy SEAL commando teams that routinely won were forced to get down on their hands and knees to half-swim, half-crawl through the quagmire. To make sure competitors didn't slink up out of the ooze and make use of the firm soil lining the drainage ditch, soldiers stood guard the length of the ditch. Just like the Raid, teams had to finish together or all be disqualified. Something about the story had convinced Burnett that I was the perfect guy to write about his Raid

Gauloises team. In fact, he'd already called the editor of *Runner's World* and told him so.

For Burnett to visualize *Runner's World* as the perfect forum to promote his team was deeply ironic, though neither he nor I realized it at the time. The roots of the Raid were the running boom of the 1970s. Some say the boom actually began with the publication of Kenneth Cooper's seminal fitness work, *Aerobics*, in 1968. Others think Americans first slipped on running shoes after Frank Shorter won the Olympic Marathon in 1972. I think it was a mixture of both: Cooper providing the kick in the ass of physiological proof that regular exercise leads to greater fitness; Shorter, the motivation by becoming the first American since 1908 to win "the ultimate test of endurance." Whatever the reason, the end result was that by 1980, the whole country was outfitted in Nike running shoes and Dolfin shorts. Before then, competitive sports focused on the notion that the athlete was a scholar (high school or college), a professional (baseball, basketball, football), a social amateur (tennis, golf, bowling), or an Olympian.

Age-group competition in endurance sports existed, but only in a very limited way. What Cooper's book and Shorter's victory did was motivate people to attempt things heretofore Herculean, like running a marathon. Once nonathletic, everyday folk learned that it was possible for them to run a mile, then a 10k, then a marathon, more than a few began looking for new endurance frontiers. The Western States, a 100-mile endurance run through the mountains of northern California, found a following. The Badwater 146, a two-day race from the lowest point in the continental United States (Death Valley) to the highest (Mt. Whitney) was begun. The "146" denotes the mileage from start to finish. In Hawaii, three guys bickered in a barroom about what was tougher—the Waikiki Rough Water Swim, the Around Oahu Bike Ride, or running the Honolulu Marathon. The result, first held in 1979, was the Ironman, a 2.4-mile swim, 112-mile bike and 26.2-mile run that spawned the sport of triathlon. But it wasn't until two years later, with a major boost from television, that the sport exploded. When ABC's *Wide World of Sports* captured top female competitor Julie Moss collapsing just before the finish line, evacuating her bowels, then crawling the final yards, America was smitten by the triathlon.

In a world of creature comforts, we were showing a deep-seated need to step outside that comfort zone. How better to feel life being lived to the fullest?

Though the Ironman was immediately given the mantle "toughest race on earth," Ironmen one-upped themselves by creating double Ironmans (4.8-224-52.4) and even triple Ironmans (7.2-336-78.6) within five years. The once-daunting marathon was looking shorter and shorter with each passing year, more a starting point for real endurance than the ultimate test.

Nonrunning endurance events began springing up. One was the Whitbread, an around-the-world sailboat race. What had been considered the ultimate sailing achievement since the beginning of time, capable of accomplishment by only the most fearless of navigators, was suddenly being attempted by doctors and insurance salesmen and sailboat bums with nothing better to do than harness themselves into a cockpit, turn on the GPS and tolerate unceasing boredom and lack of sleep, all for the sake of accomplishment. Several died underestimating the challenge.

It was while covering the Whitbread for French radio in 1987 that Gerard Fusil dreamed up the Raid concept. Noting that the Whitbread was an emulation of the expeditions of great colonial mariners, like Magellan and Drake, while watching the field navigate the treacherous waters around South America's Tierra del Fuego, he conceived of a similar expedition-based race, but taking place on land. A race without motorized transportation. A race in which the team dynamic that drove colonial expeditions to either mutiny or success could be emulated in the same extreme, uncharted circumstances. A race in which competitors would be self-sufficient, but for the safe harbor of refueling points. A race, thought the man who grew up idealizing an uncle who made his living as an African bush pilot (Fusil kept a photo of the uncle on his dresser throughout childhood), to stir the imagination and bring a sense of romance to competitive sports.

Fusil appears prescient in retrospect, but he was acting out of passion. It was pure luck that the major athletic trend of the 1990s would be "extreme" sports—rock climbing, mountain biking, mountaineering—that perfectly suited his vision of the ideal adventure. Beyond just sports, that his fledgling concept would tie in neatly with the three major themes of the 1990s—health, ecology, and the search for unconventional experiences—was a blessing. None of this could possibly have been planned by Fusil.

I can envision exactly what happened. He was at the bottom of the world covering a race in which the competitors are strung out by days and weeks. There wasn't a lot to do while waiting for the odd boat to bob past, other than make small talk with the handful of journalists and race officials on hand. Maybe he filed a few dispatches, did some journal writing, read a book. But mostly, with nothing like cable television or a local multiplex to distract, he took in the scenery. His mind wandered. The cobwebs and day-to-day distractions, the press of deadlines and the bustle of Paris, all were replaced with clarity of thought. His body got in synch with his surroundings. He began to smell the sea breeze a little more easily and clearly. The way shore birds caught a current and glided miles without flapping a wing was not only noticed, but admired. He began to set his body clock by sunrise and sunset instead of an alarm clock and dinner engagements. These sensations were all pleasurable, worth duplicating.

And as he became more and more attuned to his environment, Fusil subconsciously began searching for a way to experience that simplicity more often. A way that would dovetail with his professional life and not feel frivolous for being pursued. And, because Fusil enjoys center stage a great deal, a way that would replace even Whitbread as the event to end all events, making Fusil an adventurer extraordinaire in France.

And that—the last part, at least—is exactly what happened. After a year's planning, and the acquisition of $5 million in corporate sponsorship from the likes of Coca-Cola and sleeping bag manufacturer Lestra Sport, Fusil gathered thirty-five teams in New Zealand in 1989. They would race from one side of the South Island to another. Fusil's wife, Nelly, was co-organizer, and came up with concepts like mandatory checkpoints (CPs), team passports (small booklets carried by each team and stamped at the checkpoints to verify completion and so prevent shortcuts), and assistance points (also called headquarters, a place where teams refueled and changed gear between stages). The weather was suitably horrid for a race of extremes, with snow and rain and overflowing rivers everywhere.

Marrying the colonial expedition theme with the most modern of technologies, Fusil beamed radio and television feeds back to Paris each night. The journalist in him recognized the powerful influence of well-placed articles, so he began the tradition of flying an army of writers and photographers from Paris. To make them feel more a part of the race, each journalist is given a special Raid Gauloises correspondent's shirt (which Fusil also wears during the Raid), complete with pockets for passport, sunglasses, pens, and notes. The button-down has become a Raid staple, an insider's reminder of three weeks spent on one very wild assignment. It is treasured.

By the time Cardinal Network, a New Zealand squad, finished in five days, twenty-one hours, and thirty-six minutes, the French public was enthralled. Graphic images of "a lot of snow, a lot of rain, and a lot of pain," as Nelly Fusil remarked, helped the Raid supplant Whitbread overnight as the ultimate test of adventure and the human spirit. After all, just six teams actually finished. When Gerard Fusil announced Costa Rica as the 1990 race site, the Raid's Paris office was inundated with queries from potential competitors. "We never did any advertising," Nelly Fusil remembers. "And people were calling us all the time. People read the articles and got interested in doing the race. And since we had many, many articles, we had many, many people calling."

So began a mad dash to make Costa Rica even more extreme and more well known than New Zealand. Seeking to add a global dimension, Fusil did much more than just recruit an army of journalists to cover the race. He actually assembled a competitive team of journos from all over the world—Jon Markman's team. The mere fact that they were journalists, a bit bumbling and generally lacking in outdoor skills, rather than expert climbers and mountaineers, gave their stories an accessibility that appealed to the modern man. Markman trained to become "patient zero" in the birth of the sport in America by running alone, wearing a backpack, in the Santa Monica Mountains above Los Angeles. He learned to skydive just days before the Raid, at a military base outside Paris along with his journalist team.

They all finished, then wrote captivating articles that appeared in France, Japan, and the United States. The word spread. And a slew of regular folk—doctors, plumbers, pharmacists—entered the 1991 Raid on the South Pacific island of New Caledonia.

I wasn't the only dreamer in Southern California taken with Markman's story. Mark Burnett, reading the Sunday *Times* in bed with his wife, Diane, came upon the color picture of teams canoeing up the lush Tortugero Canal. He paused. A former soldier in the British Army who served in the Falkland Islands campaign, Burnett had more than a passing acquaintance with outdoor activity. But since leaving the service and emigrating to America there had been little chance to put it to use. Sure, he lived in wooded Topanga Canyon, north of Los Angeles. But his jobs had ranged from nanny to soccer coach to owning a company selling credit cards—anything to stay in America. His goal of fulfilling the American dream by pulling himself up by his bootstraps allowed little time for frivolous outdoor adventure.

Yet, as Burnett began reading Markman's article—then stopping and rereading it aloud to Diane—he saw something in the Raid beyond the adventure that made my imagination soar. He understood immediately how the idea of the Raid made him feel, and that others would share his enthusiasm. And then the entrepreneur in Burnett began to ponder how that enthusiasm could be translated into a financial opportunity. Was there money in the Raid's adventure?

Burnett decided that not only would he do the race himself, but he would bring a similar race to America. That began a frenzied effort to put together Team American Pride and finance the adventure by acquiring sponsors. As Burnett went from one corporation to another, polishing his sales pitch in person and on the phone, two things happened: he realized he possessed a gift for courting potential investors; and he met Brian Terkelsen, a young, long-haired former New York investment banker who'd come to California in search of a career change. The soft-spoken, introverted Terkelsen was the perfect foil for the brash Burnett.

With Burnett doing the talking and Terkelsen crunching the numbers (and doing significant research showing that the 1990s would be the decade of extreme outdoor sports and self-actualization through daunting challenge), they put together a five-year plan for the development of a Raid-style race in the United States. Eventually, the commodity would include not only a race, but also outdoor schools, motivational speeches, and product tie-ins. For all that to happen though, Burnett needed to spread the news of the Raid Gauloises to America. Americans have a natural affinity for adventure, Burnett reasoned. They just need to be reminded. Which was when he stumbled across my Volkslauf story in the May 1992 issue of *Runner's World*.

After I got off the phone with Burnett I called the editor of *Runner's World*, a business-like former Boston Marathon winner named Amby Burfoot who has a precise vision about what the average runner does and does not want to read in his magazine. I didn't think Amby would be amused by Burnett telling him who to assign to a story that hadn't even been considered for the editorial calendar. He wasn't. But just enough of Burnett's tales about the Raid's hardships and endurance requirements caught Amby's attention. In a move the likes of which I haven't seen before or since, Amby assigned me the story based on a single persuasive phone call from Burnett.

I called Burnett back and told him that because I wouldn't be covering the Raid in person, I would be relying on his accounts of the action. Keep a journal, I told him, and call me as soon as you get back.

It was mid-December 1992 the next time we spoke. Things hadn't gone as hoped. At first it had been great. Team American Pride, whose membership included a stockbroker, an aerobics instructor, a freelance television producer, and an actor, in addition to Burnett, were greeted warmly by Fusil and the French. At the prerace briefing they were given a standing ovation. Something about having Americans at the Raid made it just that much more valid in their minds as the toughest race on earth.

It was only when the Raid began that things went wrong. The first event was a twenty-five-mile ride-and-tie. Each team was given three horses. While three members rode, the other two would run as the course ascended the dry riverbed known as Wadi Akhbar. For some reason, American Pride's stubborn nags wouldn't run. The team literally pulled them the entire distance. To add insult to injury, after the roped ascent through a waterfall that began the second stage, mountaineering, the actor refused to continue unless the team stopped, built a fire, and dried their clothes. The bitter argument that followed foreshadowed the actor's eventual departure from the race three days later. Fed up with his teammates, the actor quit in mid-kayak by making an abrupt right turn and steering for shore. As Raid rules stipulate that either all five team members finish together or the entire team is disqualified, American Pride was immediately out of the competition. The remaining members could complete the race, but could not win.

The four became three six days after that when the aerobics instructor suffered a sprained ankle. Only Burnett, TV producer Susan Hemond, and stockbroker Norman Archer Hunte joined Markman as American Raid finishers.

Interestingly, Hunte almost wasn't allowed to compete because he couldn't swim. His alternate was Jim Garfield, a Chicago native who'd come west after college to pursue an acting career. The adventure of the Raid was an inexplicable siren song to this lifelong city boy. And though Hunte was reinstated after taking a quickie swim class, Garfield never ceased his drive to attempt the Raid Gauloises. Five more years would pass before that goal was realized.

Despite the difficulties, and despite the fact that American Pride finished last, three of the team members had finished. They had done whatever it took to complete the toughest race on earth. Once, down to their last swig of water, the team passed the canteen. One by one they poured the water in their mouths, swished it around, then spit it back into the canteen and passed it on to the next teammate.

When my *Runner's World* story ran in September 1993, I described the awful details of the team's split, but also the heroics of going on despite being in last place. I wrote about the Raid as an epic. Nathan Bilow's graphic photos of athletes attempting the stark mountains amplified what I was trying to say. But the American cable company broadcasting Team American Pride's exploits found themselves unable to explain to viewers in simple TV terms what exactly "Raid Gauloises" meant. Though a "raid" is an adventurous weekend to the French, and the Gauls settled what would become modern France, a cleaner, neater description was conjured: "Challenge of the Warriors."

There was no basis in fact, merely the hope that folks at home would be intrigued enough by the abstract, extreme, patently absurd title to tune in for coverage of this abstract, extreme, vaguely absurd endurance race.

The phone rang a few weeks after the story appeared. I was in my office cubicle fiddling with a budget spreadsheet, watching the clock.

"Mark Burnett here," the caller announced jovially.

We spent the first few minutes catching up. When I interviewed Burnett months before, I'd been repelled by his fondness for bluster. My opinion had softened, though. Burnett, in my opinion, was a thirty-two-year-old boy, still seeking parental approval by doing the outrageous. I found it hard to like him, but even harder to dislike him. The last time I'd seen him was at the 1993 Volkslauf, six months after he'd done the Raid in Oman. Burnett showed up wearing an all-white jumpsuit plastered with Raid patches. Not only was he not self-conscious about wearing all white to a public mud bath, but the first question he asked was where to find the Navy SEALs. They were the best of the best, he told me confidently just before the race began. If he was going to win the next Raid Gauloises, he needed a few for his team.

I pointed out a group of bare-chested, well-muscled guys hanging out at the starting line. Burnett was over there in an instant, white suit and all. I cringed for him, sure that the ultra-secretive SEALs would blow him off as a half-loony wanna-be. After the gun sounded and I slipped and slid around the course, my thoughts would occasionally go back to Burnett, and how I hoped against hope he hadn't embarrassed himself too badly. He was, after all, a pretty nice guy.

Well, I learned a lesson in dauntlessness that day. Because when I next saw Burnett after the race, white jumpsuit stained a grimy brown from cuffs to collar, he was all smiles. The SEALs were not only interested, but two had signed up on the spot.

So as I sat in my office, bored at the end of a long day, it was nice to hear Burnett's voice. Something about him spoke of opportunity. Or, failing that, dogged persistence. "I've shown your story to race officials," Burnett said finally. "They'd like to know if you're free in November to cover this year's race in Madagascar."

"I'm sure I could do a few phone interviews."

Burnett paused—I wasn't getting the picture. "It's more than that. They'd like to fly you over and have you cover the Raid firsthand. You know, actually go to Madagascar."

I don't remember what I replied, other than stammering something about getting back to him. Madagascar, I thought, hanging up the phone. Third-largest island in the world. Former French colony. Land of lemurs and vanilla plants. Located off the east coast of Africa. The farthest country on the globe from California, exactly halfway around the world. There was the chance I would sell enough stories to make the venture extremely profitable—profitable enough to quit the corporate world.

Madagascar.

This is where I was forced to face the awful realization that I was all talk. It's one thing to wish for an independent lifestyle and to succeed or fail based purely on your own merits. But actually stepping away from the corporate womb—from the benefits, regular hours, and guaranteed paycheck—why, that's working without a net. It was frightening even to consider.

So I put Madagascar out of my mind. My convenient excuse for chickening out was that it would mean leaving my wife, Calene, alone for three weeks with our three-year-old and one-year-old sons, Devin and Connor. And besides, getting time off from work would be impossible. I'd probably get fired if I tried. And what about that jungle? Madagascar's rain forests are home to all manner of reptiles, including rivers full of crocodiles. The Indian Ocean, which laps Madagascar's eastern shoreline, contains so many sharks that wading is prohibited on some beaches. As much as I wanted to travel, I didn't like the idea of my kids being fatherless because I was stupid enough to travel halfway around the world to be eaten by prehistoric beasts. Be careful what you wish for, the man said. You just might get it.

Madagascar popped in and out of my brain for a week before I mentioned it to Calene. She's the perfect sort of woman for a dreamer to marry, encouraging yet practical. Her opinion means everything to me. "The only thing I'm afraid of is that you won't have a job when you get back," she said when I finally brought it up. We were in the kitchen. I was leaning on the counter, drinking beer while she cooked dinner.

I could see Saddleback Mountain out the picture window. Halloween had just passed, the warm craziness of Thanksgiving dinner—which I would miss if I went to Madagascar—was looming, and Christmas was close enough that we'd already ordered cards.

The thought of missing a crucial chunk of the holiday countdown was discomfiting and made my decision all the tougher. So I stared at the hulking green slopes of Saddleback as a way to see a solution more clearly. In summer the mountain would turn brown, and the Southern California haze would render the nearby slopes (just four miles from my front door to the base) invisible, but now it loomed green and gorgeous after early autumn rains. Whenever I want to think, my eyes turn to Saddleback. There is something in that mountain that calls to my imagination.

Saddleback is actually two mile-high peaks, Modjeska and Santiago, side by side. But viewed from a distance they appear to be a western saddle, hence the name. The seagoing Indians that peopled Orange County centuries ago, a tribe known as the Gabrielinos, sighted on the center of the saddle to guide them back to their mainland villages after fishing expeditions off Catalina Island. Now Saddleback is protected as part of Cleveland National Forest. Its undeveloped ruggedness is a sweet contrast to the subdivisions of Orange County. When I run or mountain bike up its dusty switchbacks I'm always amazed that such pristine wilderness exists mere minutes from the cities of Orange County, as slick and modern a civilization as any on the planet. I've sorted so many nagging problems out on those long runs that the mere image of Saddleback clears my head.

So I stared at Saddleback for inspiration as I danced around the subject of primitive Madagascar. I told Calene that I'd thought about the possibility of getting fired. And about the snakes, alligators, forty-hour plane flight over four different bodies of water, and even being intimidated by working with bona fide international journalists for the first time. They were the real deal. I was afraid of not measuring up.

She listened quietly throughout dinner as I thought aloud, weighing the pros and cons. "Do you want to go?" Calene asked finally. She rested her forearms on the table and gazed intently at me. Just looking at her made me want to stay home. What sort of man leaves a beautiful, brown-eyed wife to watch obsessive-compulsives race around a back-water republic?

"Uh, yeah. Yeah, I do. This could be a once-in-a-lifetime chance to travel. I just want this to be something we agree on."

"I think you should go."

"Then . . . good. I'm going."

So I nervously asked for, and received, three weeks' time off. I marched down to the Orange County immunization center and got my shots for hepatitis and a dozen other diseases so tropical in description that merely getting inoculated made me feel like Indiana Jones. I began taking malaria pills. I bought my Lonely Planet guidebook on Madagascar and read it religiously. I got my first passport, with a suitably derelict photo. I purchased two new notebooks, one for journal keeping and another for taking race notes. Blank white pages turn me on. My new notebooks, soon to be filled with thoughts, words, and deeds from a land so strange that no one I knew had even imagined going there, dazzled me that much more.

On November 18, I boarded Virgin Atlantic flight 007 from Los Angeles to London, connecting, after a four-hour layover in London, to Mauritius via Air Mauritius, then Reunion Island and Madagascar on Air Madagascar. Every time I changed airlines the aircraft would get less modern; the flight attendants' costumes that much more exotic. But I had no way of knowing this when I boarded the flight in Los Angeles. In fact, I had no idea what I would find. Or even what I hoped to find, other than adventure and the chance to play big-league journalist. From my backpack to my boots, everything I wore was shiny new. I didn't even know how to set up my brand-new tent. I was a rookie, to be sure, out of my element. In the satchel I carried onto the plane was a small toy fire truck Devin loaned me for the trip. A Matchbox. Red, with glass in the windows. He had handed it to me impulsively the day before, reminding me that I "would need toys to play with in the jungle." It would become my touchstone.

I found my seat with the help of the British flight attendant. Sitting down, I wrote a few words in my journal, then tried to sleep, hoping all the while to wake up on another continent.

What goes through your mind when you decide to leave a safe, but unfulfilling job, and begin doing the type of work you always dreamed of? For me it was two things: First, fear. Total fear, the kind you suppress the instant it creeps up from the subconscious because it's too terrifying to face. The second was euphoria, the kind kids feel on the last day of school. "I can do anything I want," it says.

It's the euphoria of freedom. It warmed me from head to toe as 007 lifted off on that warm November afternoon. And while panic set in now and again during the journey, it finally went away. The euphoria was stronger than ever when I touched down at Antananarivo International Airport two days later.

CHAPTER 2

A Little Bit of Madness

Madagascar, 1993

"If you are attacked by a crocodile," Gerard Fusil began, peering intently into the auditorium, eyes fairly twinkling, "he will drag you under, spin you around and around to disorient you, then eat you later." It was the prerace briefing in Antananarivo, two days before teams would parachute into the Madagascan bush to begin the 1993 Raid Gauloises.

FOUR HUNDRED members of the Raid community packed the room: forty teams of competitors in uniform, fidgeting, seated by team; print journalists scribbling in new notebooks; photographers, flitting and firing, searching for the perfect angle; assistance teams; Gerard's battalion of helpers. Like an invading army, we would fly into the bush the next day to overnight at the starting line, traveling in an armada of four helicopters, two DC-3s, and a fat-bodied Russian Antonov cargo plane piloted by a Soviet capitalist named Bob. In just four years the Raid had grown from an offbeat Parisian endeavor into the French, Swedish, Japanese, Belgian, German, American, British, Saudi, and Austrian horde before Fusil. The auditorium reeked of anticipation. The auburn-haired Frenchman balled one hand into a tight fist. He leaned forward for emphasis, looking like an Old West snake oil salesman about to give away a very dear—albeit improbable—secret to the universe. "Your only defense is to shove your fist all the way into his open mouth. There is a valve there—deep in the throat—that prevents water from entering his lungs. If you can open the valve with your fist, he will begin to choke and drown." His arm was extended now, deep inside the maw of an imaginary crocodile.

"Then you can escape."

Pre-briefing speculation had held that Fusil would announce a course on Madagascar's heavily forested east coast, a tropical, mosquito-infested quagmire. Ceaseless rainfall, poisonous vipers, and a huge Indian Ocean shark population would be the biggest hindrance.

Instead, he announced, the course would go west, a march from desert to sea. The 1993 Raid Gauloises would start in the city of Mandabe, a former French colonial outpost. The order of events would be sky-diving, orienteering and climbing, canoeing, desert trekking, then ocean kayaking. With the exception of the skydiving, each stage would be between forty and 150 miles long. The course would zig-zag instead of travel in a straight line, so that map and compass skills—perhaps the most significant talent required of Raiders—could be tested by the eight to ten mandatory checkpoints during each discipline. Teams would transition from one sport to another at special "assistance points," which were also the only places where they would be allowed to seek medical assistance and resupply food stores. Finally, after at least eight days of competition, teams would finish in Ifaty, a cove just north of Toliara, where pirate vessels moored 100 years ago between attacks on shipments around Africa.

The move was vintage Fusil. In one stroke he coupled his flair for romantic surprise with the swashbuckling allure of history. Teams scrambled to make sense of their brand-new maps. The second stage appeared most difficult—seventy kilometers of climbing, rappelling, and orienteering through the Makay Massif, its sheer towering walls and craggy red rock bearing an intimidating resemblance to the Grand Canyon. Water would be scarce. Temperatures would be above 100 degrees. Competitors, Fusil said, would be lucky to traverse the Makay Massif in four days.

The favored teams scoffed. Douanes, L'Arche, and Hewlett-Packard brashly predicted they would navigate the Makay in two. It was simple land navigation, they pointed out. They felt the race would be won either during the 100 kilometers of canoeing on the Mangoky, or on the final push, a 120-kilometer ocean kayak from Andavadoaka to Ifaty.

"Do not take this lightly," Fusil tsk-tsk'ed. "You have never seen anything like Madagascar in your entire life."

Fusil hit the nail on the head. If I had searched the globe for the worst, the very worst, possible place to play out my journalistic fantasies, I couldn't have chosen any better than Antananarivo, Madagascar's capital city. The country's ruler since 1975, a communist dictator named Didier Ratsiraka, had run the economy into the ground. Per capita income was down by half. Literacy rates had plummeted. Infant mortality was at an all-time high. But those are just statistics, numbers on paper. More compelling evidence is the impoverishment of Antananarivo. It is a hole, an armpit, an austere chancre, utterly devoid of comfort and charm. It smells of wood smoke and raw sewage, a potent combination that invades the nostrils and takes up residence. What beauty "Tana" possesses is forbidding and stark, wholly uninviting.

Madagascar itself is an island, the third largest in the world (after Greenland and New Guinea), broken away from Africa 165 million years ago through the annual inch-by-snail's-pace-inch process of separation known as continental drift. Madagascar lies 240 miles east of the dark continent's closest nation, Mozambique, separated by the Mozambique Channel. It was French once, and its rotting gothic cathedrals still give Antananarivo a medieval feel, a sensation accentuated by the sight of underdressed, underfed peasants living near open sewers. Children, noses oozing green snot that no parent bothers to wipe, fight dogs for scraps of food. It has always been that way in Madagascar—under the tribal chiefs, then the French, then the military, and now the communists. There is no hint of anything resembling forward progress or upward mobility. The stench of hopelessness permeates everything. Strangely, in a land where I never once saw a basketball or basketball court, Michael Jordan T-shirts were very popular. So were Los Angeles Raiders T-shirts. I even saw "Crips," the name of a notorious Los Angeles gang, spray-painted graffiti-style in red on a brick wall.

Coming straight from the land of Taco Bells, cellular phones, and air-conditioning, my first night in Madagascar was pure culture shock. I stayed in a quaintly decomposing hotel near the airport, the Hotel Au Transit. There were flower beds outside my window. "The room is clean," I wrote in my journal, "with a pine table for writing and two single beds pushed together to make an uncomfortable double. There is no phone here, at least none that works, and I feel suddenly and completely cut off from Calene and the boys."

The red fire engine rested on my writing table. "Landing at the Antananarivo Airport there was light fog. Idle propeller planes lined the tarmac. I stepped out of the rundown Air Madagascar jet, saw the laconic soldier with the AK-47 nonchalantly watching my every movement, and felt like I had just stepped into *Casablanca*. It was all very romantic. That aura vanished after I collected my backpack and stepped outside the airport. A horde of begging children descended upon me, their dark faces unwashed, hair matted, eyes too worldly. I only had a few hundred dollars in my pocket, but I felt rich, and was embarrassed to feel that way. The taxi ride to the hotel was a journey through one slum after another, and whatever perceptions I might have had about Madagascar being an exotic treasure have been discarded. I can only hope that the rest of the country is different."

This was when a panic set in, a panic that told me I'd made a horrible decision in coming. My impetuous desire to spread my wings and step clear of the corporate world had brought nothing more than an awful glimpse of poverty and communism's grimy aftereffects. Feeling very much the international travel rookie, I slept on top of the covers that first night, wearing all my clothes to ward off bedbugs. I wondered why Gerard Fusil couldn't hold a Raid in London or Paris or Lisbon—locales equipped with museums and taverns and sidewalk cafes that served espresso until all hours. Adventure is where you find it, I thought, as I fell asleep wondering what Rome was like.

The next morning, stepping aboard the first of three airplanes that would fly the journalists from Tana to the start in Mandabe, I saw a familiar face. David Tracey is my opposite in every way, which may or may not explain why he's one of my best friends. He's a Canadian journalist who surfs and plays Frisbee more than anything else. In his spare time he writes. But where I labor over every word, spending hours on the simplest of assignments, David dashes off brilliant pieces in minutes. He's taller than I am, with shoulder-length black hair, a practiced air of nonchalance in the face of all worry, and a wonderful sense of humor that is best described as witty. The word is full of understatement, as is David.

We met in Waikiki in 1992, covering a surf lifeguard competition. Hurricane Iniki descended just after we arrived, forcing evacuation of all beachfront hotels. Calene and Devin were with me. I still have a clear image of my wife, eight very large, miserable months pregnant, pushing Devin in the stroller amid a throng of fellow displaced persons. I struggled behind like a pack mule with our diaper bag and four suitcases. David was at my side, loaded up with his own stuff, making witticisms about the boarded-up windows of downtown Waikiki, the Jack-in-the-Box restaurant where we stocked up on Breakfast Jacks in case food became scarce, and the chain-smoking Japanese tourists so practiced in group dynamics that they evacuated in straight, orderly lines. Raging wind pushed at our backs with every step. Rain wasn't falling yet, but the sky was black at mid-morning.

We found shelter in the bar of an Outrigger Hotel, three blocks from Waikiki Beach. Gradually, as time passed and the heat of the full barroom combined with boredom, David and I remembered that it was our journalistic duty to witness Iniki's landfall. Happy idiots, we fought the 125-mph winds of Iniki to the beach. Normally a tawdry, decadent patch of paradise full of trinket and T-shirt stores, it looked eerily gorgeous amid the impending chaos. Palm trees were bowed. The surf churned brown, and the air was piss warm.

Standing there, leaning into the wind like a Marcel Marceau imitator, feeling it push my hair back as if I were sticking my head out the window of a car, I felt a familiar happiness wash over me. It was the feeling of *just once*, the way all things superlative should be experienced. So that when I am old and confined to a wheelchair, and the folks in the nursing home wonder what that feeble-brained man who wets the bed ever accomplished in his lifetime, I will smile inside and remind myself of all the special things I did just once. Just once, to make life worth living. Just once I hitchhiked across the country, I rode an elephant, I took my boys to their first baseball game.

Just once I stared into a tropical hurricane.

"Get out of the street NOW, or I will place you under arrest," a Honolulu cop yelled, cruising slowly by, surveying streets without cars. David and I loped back to the hotel unscathed and unshackled, deciding that experiencing, just once, quality time in a Honolulu jailhouse wasn't really worthwhile.

David and I kept in touch by fax, tossing around story ideas and leads over the wires. To this day, when I hear of a potentially great adventure that comes with a complimentary airline ticket, I call David, and vice versa. Freelance writing is a solitary business, but journalists have to work together.

When I found out I was going to Madagascar I told him who in Paris he needed to fax in order to wrangle a plane ticket and whatever other accommodations the Raid offered. I figured that being a just-once guy would make David perfect to hang out with at the Raid. He's adventurous. He's conscientious about note-taking and interviewing. He brings an armload of paperbacks. He's not the sort to be upset about little things, which is very helpful around the French. And best of all, he sees the world as one absurdity after another. Seeing him on the 737 to Morombe was great. Just hearing the English language was a relief. I would come to rely on David in the weeks to come, as he'd traveled the world a great deal more than I (actually, as this was my first trip abroad, pretty much everyone fell into that category). David had been to places like Nepal and Tibet, and even interviewed the Dalai Lama. My treks to local triathlons fell somewhat short in this category.

LIKE THE other favored teams in the Madagascar Raid, the new Team American Pride discounted the difficulty of the Makay Massif. Burnett had disbanded the Oman team and rebuilt. Susan Hemond was still there, but three new members gave the team a competitive heft it previously lacked. Pat Harwood, Bruce Schliemann, and Rick Holman were the Navy SEAL commandos Burnett had recruited at the Volkslauf. They were trained for land, sea, and air battle scenarios. Climbing and paddling, the staples of Raid competition, were something they did every day of the year. It made them perfect Raiders.

Harwood was tallest, with blond hair, beach-boy good looks, and a penchant for referring to himself as "Fabio." Schliemann was a lean, brown-haired man with a polite undercurrent to his easygoing demeanor. He'd grown up in a foster home and I got the feeling from the way he held himself slightly distant from groups that he'd been an underdog all his life. Holman, he of the barrel chest and thick brown mustache, was team navigator. Stoic, calm under pressure, Holman was hardest to know and easiest to admire. Something about him fairly oozed unspoken confidence.

I have a photograph of our first meeting. It was taken in Mandabe, moments before the start. The air was already thick with heat at dawn. Curious villagers gathered around, looking at the airplanes and parachutes and television cameras as if we were all visitors from another planet. Team American Pride stands in a semicircle before me as I conduct a last-minute interview. About to clamber aboard a DC-3 and leap from 12,000 feet onto a high desert plain, they wear blue and gold jump suits. Susan Hemond looks distracted, but eager. The SEALs are calm. Burnett stands just out of the frame, prattling on about hopes of victory while trying to conceal thoughts of imminent pancaking. He predicted again and again that Team American Pride would definitely become the first American team to win the Raid Gauloises.

No doubt about it.

For that reason, French teams despised Team American Pride. The French are a people with a penchant for conquering the extreme. "France cannot be France without grandeur," Charles de Gaulle is reported to have said. It is home to the world's most daunting bicycle race, the Tour de France. The best single-handed sailors are almost invariably French, as are top extreme skiers and rock climbers. The Raid is an outgrowth of this lust for the epic, the grandiose. It is a source of tremendous national pride. Daily video updates are beamed back to Paris by Fusil, where they are shown on the evening news. An example of the impact: As I waited in the airport to leave Madagascar once the Raid was over, a Frenchman just off an Air France 747 from Paris gave me a blow-by-blow account of the Madagascan Raid. He knew far more about the race than I did.

Despite their reputation for aloofness, the French people I was meeting in Madagascar viewed life with one eye on wonder at all times. There is a strong sense of aesthetic to their culture. They look for the good in people and nature. Though one snide British journalist made it clear to me that the French affection for grandeur stemmed from an inability to wage war—"they can't fight, so they do the Raid"—the fact remains that the Raid Gauloises is French, through and through. Teams are expected to spend the days before the race in relaxation and community. Which is why the intensity of American Pride stood out.

Watching French teams glare daggers at American Pride moments before the start brought forth another *Casablanca* image: the scene in Rick's Café Americain where French expatriates rise and sing an emotional "Marseillaise." They are wonderful people, the French, but often proud, and can behave with a paranoia that suggests they believe the entire world is making a conscious attempt to denigrate their precious way of life. With their colonial empire gone, they cling to all they hold uniquely French, which is why I had a creeping sensation that Burnett's flagrant predictions of victory could only serve to stiffen the resolve of top French teams.

The Raid began quietly. No cannon shot, no starter's pistol. The DC-3 simply taxied out in a cloud of dust, revved its twin propellers and waited for a signal from Fusil. He stood to one side of the runway, his right arm straight up in the air, as if starting a school-yard footrace. He let it linger a minute, perhaps thinking of the year of planning and reconnaissance about to conclude. Or the week of racing about to begin. His teeth shone in a mischievous grin. Making a concentrated effort at mental recording, his head swiveled right to left, his eyes cataloging all before him—the DC-3 on the runway, the writers and photographers, the natives circling the edge of the clearing—before he chopped his arm to the ground. In a sudden flurry of noise, the plane lumbered and screamed down the dirt runway, straining to lift Fusil's Raiders toward the drop zone. As the dull gray bird took wing, Fusil looked like a child on Christmas morning.

The minimalist starting procedure set a proper tone. My mental view of the Raid was grand and glorious, a series of glossy magazine layouts. But the truth was much more severe. I would find that it's brutal and painful. Ostentation and glamour are stripped from competitors' minds within the first hour. Self-delusion vanishes soon after. It is as close to being a search for truth as anything ever devised. To call it spiritual would be to exalt it, and the Raid is far too humble for that. It is merely a test of human character, where honest motivation is divined from action.

"Do I have what it takes to finish?" was the question within each competitor. None knew, even those who'd finished before. The Raid is about looking into your soul, something modern man finds uncomfortable. We are distracted constantly by telephones and televisions, too many hours of work, and frustratingly long commutes. Modern life is not conducive to reflection, but the Raid is. By the time they arrived in Ifaty, each member of every team would have had a chance to spend countless hours inside his or her own head. There would be priority-setting questions, like whether or not work is more important than loved ones. And questions about whether or not they wanted to finish for themselves or to make a parent or wife or girlfriend proud. So it was fitting that the moment of no return was discreet. It set the proper tone.

Covered with dust from the prop wash, I threw myself into the back of a helicopter and caught a ride to the landing zone. Still in the throes of homesickness, not yet in synch with the Raid's machinations or the sun's early rising and setting, I was sweating and unenthused. The Raid's attraction, while decidedly adventurous, was lost on me. I hastily wrote in my new blue notebook: "I don't think much of the Raid, personally. Not the dirt nor the locale nor the race itself. It's a silly contrivance, putting an endurance race in the middle of these extreme surroundings. A French last bastion of colonialism. I can never see myself doing this."

My reasoning was partly a reaction to the absurdity of the event (just what, exactly, was the point?) and partly an awestruck acknowledgment that Raid competitors were truly a separate breed, a cut above. I've been an endurance athlete all my life, a runner. I ran college track and cross-country. I have run marathons and raced triathlons. I am used to the competitive ideal of pain and suffering. But the Raid . . . it boggled the mind. I lacked the inclination to hike for days without sleep. I knew nothing about rock climbing and rappelling. Ocean kayaking and canoeing are another realm of athletic competition altogether, combining seamanship with upper-body endurance. And last, I have little tolerance for team dynamics. Mostly because I'm something of a loner, but also because I'm far too thin-skinned when others criticize. I've known it since Little League baseball. So the thought of being in a situation where I'm tired, hungry, cold, wet, miserable, and surrounded by teammates struck me as a constrictive recipe for unneeded anguish. Let others do the Raid, I thought as I choppered to the landing zone, I will never have the temperament for it. Put me in the shade of a tall tree with a notebook and cold drink and I will watch.

When the first jumpers hit the landing zone, it was American Pride who landed perfectly, right on the huge chalk "X" delineating the center of the zone. While the SEALs and Susan hastily changed into the clothes they would wear for the next nine days (long-sleeved T-shirts, shorts, hiking boots, lightweight packs) a glad-to-be-alive Burnett gushed into a TV camera about how competing in the Raid was the ultimate, blah, blah, blah. He wore a laminated picture of his year-old baby boy and recently deceased mother around his neck. "This is wonderful, really wonderful. I am so thrilled to be here, to be a part of this incredible team."

"Which way do you go from here?" the TV interviewer asked. His name was Mark Steines. He would later go on to star on the television show *Entertainment Tonight*. In Madagascar, and later in Borneo, he was just making a name for himself as a formidably smooth, knowledgeable on-air reporter. At that point, he and I constituted the entire American journalistic community covering the Raid Gauloises. After Madagascar, when he screened his first Raid documentary (it would later run on ESPN and Channel 9 in Los Angeles) every single American having anything to do with the Raid Gauloises could fit in one small living room. Including spouses, the number was fewer than thirty.

"Here?" Burnett answered matter-of-factly. "From here we go southeast."

"Due west," Rick growled impatiently without looking up. He was stuffing MREs (Meals Ready to Eat) in his pack. They contained 2,500 calories in each serving, enough to fuel a normal man for an entire day. Team American Pride would eat at least five apiece in the same span.

"Right. Due west," Burnett replied, chattering on unfazed. "Due west." The answer stood as a testament to Burnett's deep need for the SEALs. In Oman he'd been the navigator and the team had spent much of the race lost. At one point, after they'd walked in circles for two days, a guide was helicoptered in by the Raid organization to show the way to the next checkpoint.

Burnett finally got his clothes changed. Team American Pride left the flat landing zone, vectoring toward the horizon, into the unknown ruggedness of the Makay Massif. The temperature was already 135 degrees—so hot that French journalists reported it ten degrees cooler in their daily feed to Paris for fear nobody would believe them. Heat shimmered off the parched plain, like stereotypical photos of the African veld. They walked separately—first the SEALs, then Burnett, and finally Hemond—spaced five yards apart. Running, or even fast walking, could prove stupid in a race lasting an entire week, so their pace was steady but not anaerobic. Moments after they disappeared over the horizon, a team of eager Parisian accountants hustled toward the Makay at a slow jog.

"Those teams that run," taunted a woman from another team as she casually slipped her chute off and pulled on her pack. For a moment I thought she was going to lie down and take a nap. "We will pass them in the night."

And they did.

I had thought that reporting the Raid would be like covering a marathon or triathlon, only with an exotic flair. There would be a press truck to cart journalists around, a helpful public relations emissary to answer questions, and possibly a large buffet at the end of the day—light snacks, hot coffee, cold cuts, stuff like that. There would be a distinct line between whatever agony the competitors were experiencing and the detached comfort required to maintain journalistic presence.

Nothing like that. Competitors and journalists are no different, enduring as one the travails of living on the wrong side of civilization. From omnipresent crocodiles and parasites to carnivorous plants, searing heat and the always petulant French, the line between us was thin. Self-preservation, not propriety, was the order of the day. Madagascar and the Raid are not places for the entitled writer.

Journalists carried their own food, water, and camping gear, just like the competitors. Like the teams, we were advised to bring a supply of food from home. If you didn't bring enough, well, you lost a few pounds and were wiser for the hardship. When asked for assistance, press liaison Antoine Le Tenneur—a young bon vivant who looked like he was born with a champagne glass in one hand—would balefully shrug his shoulders and take a long drag on his Gitanes before telling you that, although he was very sorry your stomach was grumbling, there was absolutely nothing he could do to help. And water? No, he had no way of procuring bottled water. Have you tried drinking from the Mangoky

River? It is very big and though it is brown and full of those awful little bugs, it is just right over there. . . .

The press truck was a press helicopter. Depending on space availability and time of day (helicopters couldn't fly past 10 AM, when it got above 100—not enough lift could be generated by the hot air) there were two ways of covering the event. The first option—the safe one—was the equivalent of death by boredom. This involved eschewing helicopters entirely and waiting at assistance points for teams to straggle in, which happened not at all for the first few days, then only every six or seven hours after that. That meant killing time making small talk in broken English with Frenchmen; searching for a treasured, illusory sliver of shade; rereading one of the five or six English language books available; and rearranging backpacks. All the while waiting for five very fatigued, usually French-speaking competitors to straggle over the horizon. Out of sheer boredom, writers, photographers, and video crews would descend upon them en masse, screaming questions and jockeying for the shot.

A day in the assistance point meant beating the heat by sitting up to my neck in the muddy, languid Mangoky. No matter about crocodiles. Unusual, even dangerous, the river was the only place for attaining comfort. A half-dozen journalists would sit in the shallows together, with only heads, books, and the hands supporting those books visible.

A typical conversation on those endless days went something like this: "Did you know there's a parasite in these waters that swims into your body through your asshole?" The questioner was invariably French, struggling to be polite by trying out his English.

"I didn't."

"Well there is. I thought you would want to know."

"Of course. Thank you very much."

The more adventurous option was to take my chances in the bush. That meant a better view of the competition. It entailed hitching a ride in a helicopter and going wherever it landed. Craggy mountain tops, desolate canyons, remote checkpoints with no distinguishing feature other than desolation. The rule of thumb was always to carry a backpack, because once a pilot dropped someone off, it might be days before he'd be able to come back and pick him up.

It was like footage I'd seen of the Vietnam War, or the opening sequence from *M*A*S*H*: A helo would fly in low, flare, hover, land. As soon as the skids nestled to earth, journos in twos and threes would hustle toward the open rear doors with heads low and packs slung over their shoulders. The moment the last guy was inside, we'd lift off. In Madagascar, where the roads are atrocious and the towns far apart, helicopters came to signify order, sanity, and civilization.

From the landing zone on Day One, I flew by plane to the first assistance point with David. We stayed there just one night before backtracking into the Makay in search of the lead teams.

The helicopter flight gave me my first low-level view of Madagascar's terrain. Vertical red canyon walls thousands of feet high wound snakelike below. There was little foliage, few villages, almost no people. Wild zebus, Madagascar's answer to the longhorn steer, could be spotted here and there, eating what greenery they could scavenge. They looked bony. I got the impression they didn't eat well during this, the dry season.

We roared into a long canyon and flared over an oasis. Below was an emerald lake, its shores hemmed by rock walls and lush jungle. Two white sand beaches gave it a Club Med feel. All it needed was cabanas and a portable bar. Maybe a suntan oil concession. It was one of the most beautiful places I had ever seen in my life. It was so perfect. So pure, so—

"—Lac du Croc," the pilot shouted above the roar of the engine, interrupting my reverie.

I didn't understand his French.

"Laaac duuuu Crooooc," he yelled again, as if saying it slowly could make me magically comprehend. David and I still looked puzzled. I tried to figure it out. *Lac*, I thought, that probably means lake. *Du*, of. *Croc* . . . of course, Crocodile Lake. The lake's beauty immediately turned deadly and unappealing. There are no more Edens, I thought. Later I was informed that two crocodiles had been spotted sunning themselves on those pristine beaches just the day before.

The pilot dropped us off in a dry creek bed in a deep, red-rock canyon. Lac du Croc was on the other side of a tiny patch of dense bamboo jungle, connected by a ribbon of barely visible trail. It was only 100 yards, maybe more, but far enough that I didn't have to worry about crocodiles slipping into my tent while I slept.

"Hullo," Julian Loader called out as we schlepped our packs from the landing area to the camp site. Julian was a British freelance writer and photographer. He wore Mr. Spock sideburns, bikini underwear and rarely anything else. Umberto, an Italian journalist with lean features, was there as well, making eyes at a real estate agent from Santa Barbara. Her hobby was adventure travel. She had paid her way to the Raid to see for herself what it was like. Vivian was in her mid-forties, wore make-up and eye liner despite the heat, and even perused a text on Eastern philosophy by the campfire, all of which made her stereotypically Southern Californian. But she turned out to be warm and kind instead of vacuous, and when we talked our conversations always turned to children. Vivian had two, like me. Boys. Her marriage had just broken up, and I gathered it was her decision. Though she said it was all for the best, she seemed terribly sad. Her words frequently trailed off in mid-sentence, as another thought or memory collided. I got the feeling her exotic travels were a front for something deeper, that like myself she was looking for something to make her whole.

We pooled our food that night, sharing what little we had and making a veritable feast over the small fire. I contributed red beans and rice. David, canned vegetables. Julian had no food, but plenty of rum. It was a joyous, relaxing evening. We sat by the fire as the sun set, getting mildly drunk and watching the rim of our gorgeous, twisting canyon get painted a delicate reddish purple. The stream trickled nearby, bringing tranquillity. We swapped stories and bitched about the French and reveled in the weird wonder of being in this remote corner of this remote country in this remote corner of the world.

"I am probably the first Canadian ever to see this canyon," David said. It was the first time I ever heard him hint at braggadocio, which gave his words additional meaning. I wondered if I was the first American, and reveled in the vague wonder of it all. These are wonderful people, I told myself in the rum's glow, looking at my fellow journalists.

It was what I had come to Madagascar for, I realized. Not to write my story, not even to watch the Raid Gauloises. And not even for a Mutual of Omaha's *Wild Kingdom* gander at beauty and adventure and majesty. What I was looking for was to belong, to find people like me. Everybody wants a place where they fit in. I was just unaware that I needed to find that place so badly.

I crawled into my tent feeling that the Raid was the perfect spot in the world for me to be. I stretched out atop my brand new sleeping bag. A handful of tentative, soothing raindrops pattered against the tent. It was good to be dry and warm. I thought of Calene, not homesick for her as much as hungry for her. I hadn't thought of sex since that first night in Tana, but it was on my mind as I drifted off just a stone's throw from Lac du Croc.

There were women at the Raid. David and I called them the fashion models. And like some taunting French reminder that aesthetic beauty is absolutely necessary to balance abject hardship, the fashion models were drop-dead gorgeous. Fusil brought them along to assist in day-to-day operations. In exchange for manning checkpoints, assisting the press, or running errands for Gerard, they received a free trip from Paris to Madagascar. Many had been doing it for years, using the Raid as their annual holiday. "I always come to ze Raid," pointed out Fanny, a busty Parisian real estate agent who prattled on endlessly about her Italian boyfriend but flirted as if he didn't really exist. "It is a wonderful way for me to see ze world."

"Thank God for that," David mumbled in awe as she walked away after that first meeting at an assistance point, doing a rumba with Rubenesque hips.

I fell asleep, and dreamed of airplanes. Big airplanes, with deafening engines, like the B-52s from the Air Force bases I grew up on. We always lived near the flight line, and mechanics working on engines would run them at all hours of the night. But this sound was even closer. As if I were standing on a runway, I could hear the engines roaring at full throttle. I tried to shut out the intrusion. I struggled to rewind to an earlier dream about swaying hips. But the roar continued, growing louder and more emphatic. The hips made a brief return appearance then slipped away, painting my dream with sudden regret. The annoying roar returned. It grew louder. Voices could be heard above the roar. Odd. Then the scurry of urgent footsteps and a hurried dragging of equipment along with the roar and the voices.

Which is when I woke up to bedlam outside my tent. I fumbled for my boots in the darkness, slipped them on and scrambled into the night without lacing them. Rain immediately beat my hair flat. Wind pushed at me, making it hard to stand, and threatened to topple my tent altogether.

I bumped into David first. "Look at that," he said, sounding almost frightened. The others huddled in the shade of a tree. Not all of them had been sleeping in tents when the rain came. In the interest of saving weight many hadn't brought one from home. They were soaked.

The jet engine roar was our docile creek, now ripping past at flash flood levels. High and roiling, the water churned, a muddy beast unloosed. It thundered through our quaint canyon. The bank was just three feet from my tent and getting closer by the minute. Had I been sleeping in the canyon alone I might not have awakened at all. I would have been swept away in my sleep.

I moved the tent back ten feet, though that wouldn't matter if the river kept rising. There would soon be no more room, no place else, to move it. It was hard to talk above the noise, so David and I just stood and watched, knowing that if the river came higher we had only one method of escape: to the rear.

To Lac du Croc.

We mentally prepared to evacuate, to race from one nightmare to another. The water continued to creep higher, its waves almost surreal in their dark brown fury. David and I made weak jokes, awful black humor about the ludicrous impossibility of shoving fists and other body parts into the mouth of a crocodile. What worried us most about retreating to Lac du Croc wasn't the lake itself, but the small natural canal in the middle of the jungle feeding into it. The canal was waist deep and dark black, even in the daytime. We had walked through it during the day (twice, on the way to and from an exploration of Lac du Croc). But walking through those opaque waters at night would be an exercise in terror. I had visions of attack by crocodile (which made my hand curl into an involuntary fist) or the slow squeeze of a boa constrictor. I saw myself getting pulled underwater and drowned, never to be found, except by other predatory underwater animals hoping to nibble my remains. It was a worthless place to die, I told myself, totally, utterly worthless.

The irrationality of my fears reached its high point at the same time as the stream. An hour before dawn, the rain stopped. The creek slowly lowered. Those without tents found room to sleep with those who did, if only to protect themselves from the possibility of a second storm.

In the morning the creek was nothing more than a trickle again. I struck my tent and ambled to the campfire. Umberto was making coffee. Vivian was there, too.

She edged close to the flame. I stood to Umberto's distant right, sipping black instant coffee. She stood to his close left. He glanced timidly at her, as if she had the power to banish him from the campfire. He smiled nervously, edged even closer. Still, it wasn't hard to hear when he cooed in her ear. "You and me, we make a beautiful memory last night."

Vivian still lives in Santa Barbara. She writes books about personal spirituality now. I got a flyer not too long ago for a self-empowerment seminar she was leading. Her picture's at the top of the page. She looks unafraid and slightly all-knowing, but in a good way.

I wonder how the Raid changed her. Perhaps, in the adventure of the flash flood and the near evacuation to Lac du Croc, she discovered some sort of new ability within herself to function under pressure. Maybe it was empowering. All I know is she was different after that, full of inner strength. In a most offbeat way, she'd found what she was looking for from the Raid Gauloises.

I began looking at the Raid with different eyes after Lac du Croc. It wasn't silly or self-indulgent at all. There's something to be said for every man or woman—whether competitor or journalist—using the Raid's adventures and hardships to come to grips with who they really are.

THE LEAD teams took almost four days to emerge from the Makay Massif. It was Thanksgiving Day back in America, but I wrote about the team's arrival with a deep hunger in my stomach and a low sun scorching the back of my neck. Drops of sweat ran down my wrist, onto my fingertips, onto my pen, then onto the page, making the ink bleed: "10:03 AM. At last, the first team is arriving, marching abreast across the mile-wide sand bar leading to the first assistance point. Shimmering heat makes the entrance all the more dramatic—as if they are a mirage. The sky is cloudless, blue, hot.

"Jura is the name of the team. Most everybody at the assistance point is marching out to them. Fusil's face looks lined and weary as he steps forward to shake their hands. Jura enjoys the attention after four days of isolation and hardship. Though their clothes are filthy and their bodies sunburned wherever clothing does not cover, they revel in their moment and answer questions with all the nonchalance of rock stars.

"In contrast, a German team who quit last night and had to be helicoptered in were too upset to answer questions. It was very sad. When their helicopter landed just after sunset, they immediately got off and limped into the darkness. By morning they had fled back to Tana, where they could sit in the air-conditioned passenger lounge of the airport, drink clear bottles of water, and await the airplane home."

Jura's position was the big surprise of the Raid so far. Led by a sad-eyed man named Bernard Dahy, Jura (named for the tiny French province from which they hailed) had started the race with a decided disadvantage: they were too poor to afford parachutes. Instead, Fusil offered them the option of walking the forty kilometers from Mandabe to the landing zone. Inconceivably, by the end of the first day they had pulled into the top ten. Within two they were in the lead. "It is simple," explained Dahy. "We don't sleep very much and we try to navigate very well. That way we don't get lost."

Their secret weapon was experience: Jura had done every Raid since the very first one in New Zealand in 1989. They wanted desperately to win, and planned their year around competing. Through accumulated knowledge of the event's pitfalls, they were able to circumvent the Raid's inherent treachery. Each member knew what it was like to walk for days on end with feet raw from blisters, and to kayak or canoe way past the moment deltoids and trapezius began to burn. Others weren't as fortunate. Horror stories were floating out of the Makay of teams falling apart as the sun baked their brains. Hewlett-Packard was one such group, stranding their female member atop a towering butte. "You are a bitch," they said before rappelling down, "we will go on without you."

Thirteen teams quit in the first two days.

Team American Pride's Burnett and Schliemann both suffered from the heat. Burnett felt woozy on the first day and Schliemann was forced to carry his pack. As a result of the extra effort, when the team ran out of water and had to backtrack twelve hours in search of more, Schliemann passed out twice from heat exhaustion. "I'm alright, I'm alright," the embarrassed SEAL would say, climbing to his feet.

"No, you're not," self-appointed team doctor Hemond would reply, forcing him back to the ground, "you can barely talk and your eyes are almost rolled back into your head."

Still, American Pride was just six hours back of Jura, in fifth place. They were the one team that each French journalist knew about on a moment-by-moment basis.

"How's Team American Pride doing?" I would ask, wandering into the race headquarters tent. It was canvas, tall, filled with communications gear. With the intense heat and nonporous canvas, the HQ tent felt like a sauna.

"Fifth," a half-dozen voices would say at once. They didn't sound happy about it. Six hours is nothing at the Raid. American Pride could move into first place at any time.

Jura began the canoe section first, with Dahy deferring to the team's paddling specialist as team leader. The Mangoky was running unusually low because of the heat. The current, which raged torrentially during the rainy season, dawdled. Teams would not have the luxury of an easy cruise down the river, they would have to paddle every bit of the way. Second-place Europe 2 arrived from the Makay Massif ten minutes behind Jura, but began the canoeing almost two hours back. As they pulled away from the bank in fresh clothes, and with eyes shiny-happy from plates of hot food and deep drinks of bottled water, their assistance team began a serenade to one of the team's two women. Sung in French, but recognizable in any language, was "Happy Birthday." The surprised woman perched in her canoe, happily on the verge of tears, thrilled that people remembered her special day amid the chaos.

In a world where little things like clean socks and food without sand make a huge difference, the song was a gigantic motivator for Europe 2. Their paddles caught the water just a little sharper after that. Their fatigue was just that much less noticeable. Jura's lead, I sensed, was by no means safe.

Through a map-reading blunder just before exiting the Makay, Team American Pride began the canoeing leg almost a full day behind

Jura and Europe 2. The error didn't dash their hopes of winning, but splintered their camaraderie. No longer were they a team, but five individuals struggling to get from start to finish without killing each other.

Hemond, who was suffering from internal bleeding, kept to herself. She cried as they marched into the assistance point. Burnett either chattered ceaselessly or kept stone silent. Schliemann, the team scout, walked 100 yards in front, listening only to his own thoughts. And Holman and Harwood shared leadership duties, though Holman pulled Harwood aside and chewed him out thoroughly for the map error. It was the one time Holman had allowed Harwood to chart their course. It would not happen again.

Another cause for concern was the rotten condition of their feet. After hiking night and day in alternately searing and soaking shoes, every member of Team American Pride suffered from blisters, black toenails, and immersion foot. The soles of their feet were white and wrinkly, as if they'd soaked in water for days. When Team American Pride walked out of the Makay and finally plopped into their assistance tent, the first order of duty for team trainer Dick Dent, Susan's fiancé, was to clean, disinfect, and tape battered feet.

With only canoeing, a cross-desert march, and ocean kayaking still to come—four days of racing, tops—American Pride's chances of winning were growing slim. Still, paddling is a SEAL specialty. The team had high hopes they could catch the leaders by the end of the canoe stage. If that failed, they planned on marching straight through the desert section—sleep be damned. "We can do it," reasoned Harwood, before adding in a low rumble, "but Fabio will be very tired."

Waiting at assistance point 2 (AP2) for Jura and Europe 2 to finish the canoeing stage, David and I were seated near the bank of the Mangoky. It was dusk. Unlike AP1's sand bar, AP2 was lunar landscape— all pitted, rocky riverbank surrounded by barrel-girthed baobob trees and leafless thorn bushes. Total, utter desolation. A river before us, a desert behind. Beyond the desert was sea, but that was so far off as to be unimaginable. The Raid's length, we were finding, was stupefying. Day after day after day after day after day of racing, with no end in sight. To make matters worse, we were without helicopter transport because there was no place among the trees and bushes to land. Stuck, we sat in sheer boredom in the river for two days, waiting for teams to arrive so we could flee by four-wheel drive to the next assistance point.

Neither David nor I, who had gotten in the habit of pooling food-stuffs, had as much as a crumb of bread left. Both of us had plenty of cash, but money is of no value when there's no place to buy anything. We were surviving on PowerBars, a carbohydrate-rich energy bar favored by competitors, that had the unfortunate side effect of total constipation. And though I knew this could be remedied if I drank at least eight ounces of water with each bar, it was hard to bring myself to choke down another swallow of bug-infested Mangoky mud. It had actually gotten worse at AP2, as a herd of zebu lived just upriver and used the Mangoky as a private toilet. Their turds floated by, sometimes bouncing into the faces of those sitting in the water.

A native wearing a Magic Johnson T-shirt had appeared out of nowhere that afternoon, selling bottles of Guinness stout and Coca-Cola. I bought two of each, even though they were hot to the touch from sitting in the sun. David bought his allotment as well. We drank on a small bluff above the river as the sun fell. We could see the usual contingent of journalists in the water, reading.

I saw Fanny before David did. She stepped from her tent in a silver one-piece bathing suit, clutching a bar of soap in her left hand. She walked at first, picking her way barefoot across the rocky soil, then began jogging. Her breasts swayed with each footfall. Thousands of miles from home and wives, David and I watched in a unique state of despair, longing, and fascination.

Without so much as a "Salud," Fanny stepped in before the readers. They stopped reading. She dunked herself under, then stood upright. The muddy river came to a point well below her waist. Slowly, Fanny peeled off one strap, then another, wriggling her suit lower and lower on her torso until it settled just below the waterline. She lathered herself slowly and casually, showing no more concern or haste than if she were under a hot shower in Paris. Then, when the suds finally covered her, she dipped under once again, rinsed it all off, pulled up her suit, and walked back to her tent—all as if nothing of consequence had occurred. Looking wistful and tormented, the readers watched her go.

"You know," David said in a near whisper, taking a pull on his hot, bitter beer. He wasn't looking at me but at a point in space far across the river. "I miss my wife."

An hour later I walked a mile downstream to take my own bath. It was a private spot, a small beach surrounded by low shrubs. I stripped, checked for crocodiles, stepped into the water and promptly dropped my bar of soap. It was impossible to find, so I made do the best I could with repeated dunkings and vigorous body rubbing, all the while dodging the floating isles of zebu surprise. Finally, convinced that I had cleansed as well as possible, I stepped from the river to towel off. This came as a great surprise to the Madagascan family that was, at that very moment, stepping from a grove of baobob trees for a walk along the riverbank. Father, mother, a boy and a girl. They all stared at me with grave curiosity. I remembered a local woman I had spoken with a few days earlier. She told me through an interpreter that I was the first white person she had seen in thirty-five years.

Now, with an entire family staring at my anatomy, I had the sensation that I had never been so naked or so white in my entire life.

JURA FINISHED the canoeing at 8:36 AM on Day Six. Because of crocodiles, paddling at night was forbidden, so they had managed a solid night's sleep for the first time since the start. The effects showed. They looked rested. Smiling. Laughing. Bernard Dahy, who looked like death warmed over after emerging from the Makay Massif, still looked drawn, but not as tired. After not cracking the top ten in previous Raids, Dahy had the obvious bearing of a man who felt his lead was tentative. It wore on him, but at the same time filled him with hope. "I am ready for the party," he said cautiously, referring to the post-race awards ceremony.

Dahy and Jura's other three men stripped down as soon as they set foot in their assistance tent. Whoosh, the clothes came off, with no regard for personal modesty. What mattered was rinsing off, changing clothes, eating a meal, and resuming the race. They stood naked for all the world to see, toweling their privates as if in a locker room. Bug bites could be seen dotting Dahy's behind as French video did an interview, but otherwise he looked good. "We are all OK," he said, "and very happy."

Unlike Team American Pride, Jura had no foot problems whatsoever, having avoided them by soaking the soles of their feet in a combination of formaldehyde and dog paw toughener in the months before the race. As a result, they didn't need to waste time with foot taping and medicating. After a change of clothes and a hot meal, Jura marched away from the river and into the desert for the final hike to the sea.

Interestingly, the Madagascans didn't refer to the maze of sticker bushes and sand as a desert. To them it was a forest. The Mikea Forest. Jura entered the Mikea at 10 AM, less than an hour and a half after finishing the canoe.

Europe 2 finished the canoeing at 10:22. They looked happy to be done, but infinitely more tired than Jura.

American Pride made up two hours during their first day of paddling. They were in fourteenth place, just twenty-two hours behind. A single wrong turn or missed water stop by Jura, and American Pride could be right back in the race.

I left the cratered world of AP2 late in the morning of Day Six. David stayed behind to wait for a Japanese team he was covering. I traveled on my own once again, with nobody to bounce ideas off of or share books with. Six journalists, plus gear, crammed into a battered four-wheel-drive minibus and took the main highway due west to the coast. The "highway" bore no resemblance to the concrete ribbons that grid America. "Beautiful country, Madagascar," a jowly South African had warned at the airport bar in Mauritius, "but no bloody infrastructure." Antoine promised there would be food for sale at the coast, however, and I was prepared to drive over a thousand miles of washboard in order to eat. PowerBars, for all their nutritional value, were no longer remotely palatable.

The road was dirty, rutted, potholed, bumpy, obnoxious, almost nonexistent. Watching people try to sleep through it was like watching marionettes—heads bobbed up and down to the rhythm of the bouncing car. The minibus reeked of body odor. Despite the heat, I was alarmed to notice that I wasn't sweating, the result of my reluctance to drink river water. My skin was mottled with patches of salt. My thirst was as strong as if I'd just run a marathon.

The landscape was unceasingly monotonous, all thorny coastal scrub and cactus. The horizon was limitless and flat, like America's Great Plains. The simplicity of the scenario fit my mood, however, and I was content to watch mile after listless mile roll past. I am by nature impatient, the type of guy who defines his day by quantifiable accomplishment. The Raid had taken away my lifelines to civilization—telephones, personal transportation, schedules—and replaced them with simplicity. I rose with the sun, scratching the sand fleas from my skull. My days were spent reading, writing, hiking, and engaged in conversation—all naturally contemplative activities. I walked with teams sometimes, bringing my parallel Madagascan experience in synch with theirs long enough to get a feel for their motivations. Each night, I unrolled my sleeping bag as soon as it got dark. Sometimes I would lie awake for hours, looking at the million unfamiliar stars of the Southern Hemisphere twinkling above.

While painful, lack of food had also increased the aura of simplicity. I was totally in tune with my body and surroundings. My thought process was clear and focused, devoid of self-deception. The daily panic to achieve and the hourly need to gobble food to fuel that panic (like a child, in times of crisis I turn to food for nurturing) were simultaneously lifted by Madagascar's isolation. I would revert to old ways once I went back home, of this I was positive, but I was enjoying the honesty of my suddenly simple days.

I smelled the ocean before I saw it, the salt air wafting like an incongruous olfactory mirage over the stark desert. Our rolling deodorant test factory became more bearable as sea aroma filled it and the outside air temperature cooled. There is a theory that the negative ions present in moving water somehow react with the body's metabolism to improve disposition, and I saw it at work that day. Sleeping heads lifted with curious expectation. Tentative smiles replaced miserable frowns. Nobody had spoken for several hours, but suddenly our little bus was filled with words and accents. Antoine rambling in Parisian French, Gitanes perched between thumb and forefinger. Umberto speaking Italian-accented English with Julian. Lars, the Swede who disparaged the Raid as a "circus" and boasted that his next adventure would be snowboarding down Mount Kilimanjaro, was asking me—we had never spoken before—if I thought we might find a seafood restaurant for lunch. He mumbled of lobster and mussels, clams and prawns, drawn butter and thick bread for dipping.

My empty stomach roared to life. It began to dream, imagining the succulence of fresh seafood. My ideals and glorification about the discipline of simplicity became an afterthought. My stomach lusted—demanded—fulfillment, and I was powerless to rein it in. "Antoine," I called out, trying not to get my hopes up. He was sitting in the passenger seat up front. "Will there be anyplace good to eat when we get to Andavadoaka?" That was our final destination, the home of AP3 and start (at last!) of the final leg, a 120-kilometer ocean kayak down to Ifaty.

Antoine, who has the sleepless circles under his eyes of a man who enjoys the night life, pulled mournfully on his cigarette. "We will not be in Andavadoaka until tonight," he said.

A wave of depression swept the bus—it was only noon. "But," Antoine added, his timing perfect, "in Morombe there will be restaurants. We are almost there." He raised one eyebrow. "I am told there will be running water and cold beer."

Running water! I tried to imagine what it would be like to wash my face in clear tap water. And cold beer! Christmas come early. We had only been away from civilization a week, but deprivation had been thorough enough that the simplest amenities seemed too luxurious for kings. Every eye peered out the windshield, watching for that one final turn in the road that would signal our return to civilization.

Another hour and we were there. Morombe wasn't much to look at, a ramshackle adobe ghost town straight out of the Old West. I had initial doubts that there would be a restaurant. But when I walked into Le Croix de Soud ("The Southern Cross") I knew that I was beginning the ascent to civilization. Though still a week away, the flight home felt just around the corner. "After hell," I wrote in my journal, "it was a blessed place." There were tablecloths, silverware, and soap and water to scrub up with in the bathroom. The water ran both hot and cold, without a trace of mud. The distinction between competitors and journalists was suddenly vast, as we enjoyed luxury while they were dropping farther and farther into a vat of deprivation and personal suffering in the Mikea Forest.

We gorged ourselves: frosty liters of the too-heavy national brew, Three Horses Beer; lobster salad with vinaigrette; a main course of bread, rice, and sautéed shrimp. By the time we piled back into the bus for the last two hours into Andavadoaka, we were all too stuffed to speak. I fell asleep immediately and dreamed of sleeping in my own bed.

Antoine awoke me in Andavadoaka, to scenery beyond magnificence. Andavadoaka was a fishing village. Simple thatched huts lined the white sand beach. Demure waves, the result of a barrier reef a mile offshore, lapped the coast. The ocean was as clear and blue as the California sky on the Fourth of July.

A half-mile south of the village, set up on a low cliff atop a horseshoe-shaped cove, was a small resort whose proprietors catered to South African sport fishermen. This would be our campsite. There was a restaurant, a bar, picnic tables, and small wooden bungalows for those wishing to sleep with a roof over their heads. A statue of the Virgin Mary stood on a rock high above the cove, her serene face gazing out to sea.

I pitched my tent on the beach, then went for a swim, carefully watching for sharks, the latest predator on the Raid hit parade. Still, I felt I was in paradise, and closer to home than at any time since I left.

This is when I learned a hard lesson about foreign currency. I had plenty of American dollars, but had resisted changing too much into Madagascan francs when leaving Tana. Hard currency is coveted in Madagascar. Their franc is so devalued that money cannot be re-exchanged when leaving the country. The last thing I wanted going home was a pocketful of worthless Madagascan money. I had reasoned I would change dollars for francs as I needed them. What I hadn't anticipated was how far from civilization and its money-changing institutions we would stray.

I had spent the last of my Madagascan money bellying up to the trough at La Croix de Soud, and there was no place in Andavadoaka to change more. I'm not above borrowing money, but after a few discreet inquiries I got the feeling francs were being hoarded. No one wanted to be without.

The moon rose directly behind the Virgin's head that night, forming a momentary supernatural halo. Just twelve hours after La Croix de Soud, I fell asleep famished, close enough to the lobster restaurant to hear the rattle of utensils and the reverie of satisfied diners.

"I THINK," Gerard Fusil mumbled, his eyes sunken and red-rimmed, "that this year we finally make a Raid that is too hard."

At 4:30 AM, under a husky yellow moon, the organizer watched Europe 2, Jura, and a surging Team Saky set out on the last of the Raid's five stages. From Andavadoaka Bay they would paddle neck-and-neck through the next day to the finish in Ifaty. And just as the blissful calm of the predawn bay was a sharp contrast to the chaos in the fatigued minds of the lead teams, so also it belied the deep worry in Fusil's. With the end close at hand, the delayed shock of near-calamity was overwhelming him.

Early on, he was the fearless leader, referring to the weather only as "unseasonably hot," even though three teams abandoned on Day One alone with heat exhaustion. By Day Three drinking water was worth more than the already devalued currency and dusk's cool winds were anticipated with a fervor reserved for national holidays. Through it all, Fusil never showed despair. The ever-confident shepherd, he took to the sky each morning with Pappy, his personal helicopter pilot, to round up the strayed and stricken. Finally, in Andavadoaka, where water was plentiful and the dashing Parisian should have allowed himself to revel in the weird majesty of his anachronistic event, he was not able to. "Safety is our main business," he finally admitted, watching the leaders head out to sea. With the full moon, calm bay, and silhouetted paddlers, the scene looked like a photo I might have hung on my cubicle wall back at the office, dreaming someday of experiencing it in person. "Nobody has ever died at the Raid, but this year we come very close."

The Mikea Forest had been the turning point in his denial. Despite the heat, he had assured teams they would be able to drink their fill halfway through the Mikea at a place known as Lake Ihotry. It was huge, he told them, and beautiful, an oasis, filled with clear green water and flaming pink flamingos. Instead, Jura found only an algae-filled puddle and acres of parched earth. Lake Ihotry was as dry as Death Valley in June. A panicked examination of the maps showed no other water source for fifty miles in any direction.

To prevent the possibility of death by heatstroke, Fusil ordered bottles of drinking water airlifted into the Mikea Forest. The top ten teams were able to resupply and make it safely to Andavadoaka. "The conditions are so bad," Fusil rationalized, "that people are tired before they are really exhausted. Last year we had two people collapse because they were so exhausted. This year we didn't have that problem—the heat was so bad that people quit before they could collapse."

Moments after the kayaking began, Fusil received word by walkie-talkie that there wasn't enough water to service teams that hadn't yet arrived at Lake Ihotry. Sadly, he gave the order to helicopter them all to the coast. Almost fifteen teams would not be allowed to complete the Mikea Forest section and would be cheated the satisfaction of completing the entire Raid. "They do not agree," Fusil said with a shrug, "but that is just like a competitor. The definition of a competitor is someone who does not agree."

American Pride was not one of the affected teams. By marching forty hours without sleep, they had pulled all the way up to sixth place when they arrived in Andavadoaka just before midnight on Day Seven. Because of the barrier reef, which hove out of the water like a coral fence when the tide was out, they wouldn't be able to begin kayaking for Ifaty until 4:30 AM, exactly twenty-four hours after Jura. They were overtired, and wanted to sleep but could not. By the light of the full moon, Harwood slumped to the beach cuddling a warm liter of Coke. "Fabio is tired," he moaned. "Very, very tired."

A tight-lipped Hemond and a shivering, chattering Burnett, who feuded all through the Mikea Forest, calling each other awful, anatomically explicit names, made their way to the beach to wash. Schliemann, already thin to begin with, had burned off all his body fat as an energy source. He looked cadaverous, with ribs and jaw pressing out sharply from his skin. "I'm really tired, man," he whispered to Holman.

Disregarding fatigue, however, American Pride was fine. Flawless navigation through the Mikea Forest by Holman had raised morale immeasurably. Overcoming the thorny Mikea and its rigorous navigation in one swoop was a major accomplishment. Victory was out of the question, not with Jura a full day ahead. But a top-five finish was well within reach, and would show the Raid world that America had the capability to be a threat in Raids to come.

It was an hour before they fell asleep. And two more before it was time to rise for yet another day of racing. When the tide finally came in and they paddled out to sea at 5:04 AM, Fusil leaned over to me and said in a confidential, revelatory manner: "Your Team American Pride has gotten better this year. They are a wonderful surprise."

Fusil and I had never spoken before that moment. We hadn't even had occasion to acknowledge each other's existence. So I was slightly floored when he addressed me in fluent, singsong English. And though it wasn't really *my* American Pride—I found the name appallingly jingoistic, even more so because Burnett is a Brit—I must admit that I felt, well, proud that Fusil had seen fit to confide in me about their performance.

Feeling a sudden kinship with my French hosts, I bummed some francs off Antoine, promising to pay him back as soon as we reached some semblance of civilization. He shrugged and puffed on his Gitanes, intimating that he didn't believe me—personal experience telling him that loans made in foreign countries are usually forgotten— but that it was OK just the same. For 5,000 francs (about $2.50) I had fresh lobster and hot coffee for breakfast, then spent the morning following American Pride and three other teams down the coast in a Boston Whaler, motoring powerfully through the sun-kissed surf, hanging on for dear life as the boat was entirely airborne between swells. It was all very thrilling, and my emotions soared (just once, I rode a motorboat in the clear blue ocean off the coast of Madagascar, where pirates once roamed).

I rose at dawn the next day and caught a helicopter to Ifaty to watch the finish. It was a beautiful morning and my resolution to see the world through less victimizing lenses had lasted through the night. Just two things were on my mind as we flew: Who would win the Raid? And, never drink three liters of Three Horses Beer in one night ever again. It makes for a foggy morning.

12:37 PM. Day Eight. Walking their boats through the briny muck of a low tide beach, water splashing their ankles like a handful of MacArthurs, Jura, the team from the tiny alpine province, finishes their victorious march from desert to sea. They dawdle, victory assured. Team Saky, which has finally passed Europe 2 on the kayaking leg, isn't even on the horizon. The finish line is as inconspicuous as the start—

merely two flags stenciled with the Raid Gauloises logo—the name of the race superimposed on a globe. Gerard Fusil walks out to meet them, shaking hands with a still sad-faced Bernard Dahy, peering into those hangdog eyes with an admiration kings once reserved for conquerors. Or Stanley, greeting Livingstone.

Champagne is produced and, after spraying his team, then the press—I can still feel the sticky sweet droplets falling on my forearms as I tried to take notes—Dahy drinks from the bottle. It is a slow drink, long awaited. "Perfect," he says in English. "Super."

The team breaks into spontaneous song, something in French about the wonders of Jura, sort of a provincial anthem. Dahy looks positively giddy for once, and when the singing stops he wraps his arm around the man he says is responsible for their success. His name is Bernard Brégeon, and Dahy recruited him for his team because he felt—justifiably so— that the race would be won or lost during the paddling stages. Brégeon, a two-time Olympic medalist at the 1984 Games in flatwater kayaking, drove the team hard during the grueling thirty-two-hour paddle from Andavadoaka, reminding them again and again that no lead is safe in the Raid Gauloises.

Brégeon smiles. He is a compact man, with taut muscles and a curt stoicism. "Right now," he says, shrugging off Dahy's compliments, though he is clearly touched, "I just want to drink something cold and eat something."

The victory party moves out of the brine up the beach to the large oceanfront resort Fusil decided was a perfect finish to his Raid. It is another of his idiosyncrasies, that he likes to balance heaven and hell. Competitors are shown the splendor of the host country at the finish line, especially hot showers, warm beds, and the glories of refrigeration.

I caught up with Dahy an hour later, reclining in the shade, probably five minutes away from an uncontrollable urge to sleep. There was a question—an obvious one, but pressing nonetheless—that I absolutely needed to ask him. Watching the finish, I found myself captivated. It was so pure, so unpretentious. Sure, there is attendant publicity in being a Raid champion, especially a French Raid champion. But the look on the face of each member of Jura as they finished—a serenity I have never witnessed in competitors ever, anywhere—was almost spiritual. It was happiness in its most undiluted form, and it sucked me in. For the first time I found myself wondering what it would be like to finish.

I cozied up to Dahy, sitting across from him on a large wicker beach chair. The air-conditioned bar was a short walk away, but he looked content to be outside, drinking warm coke from a liter bottle. I introduced myself, looked him in the eye, and asked him my probing question.

"Why in the world do you do this race?"

Dahy had heard it a million times before. "The spirit of the competition," he said, "and a little bit of madness."

RACE OVER, my job complete, I fled Madagascar the next morning, well before American Pride finished. While I was flying in a Cessna from Ifaty to Antananarivo, seeing Madagascar from 1,200 intimate feet, they were suffering the delayed effects of total exhaustion. Hemond, who had lost fifteen pounds, hallucinated, sure that she saw condominiums lining the Madagascan coastline. They all took turns falling asleep in midstroke. They finished ninth, over twenty-four hours after Jura.

I wasn't there when Gerard Fusil welcomed them ashore just past sunset on Day Nine, lighting a red flare to announce their arrival. And I wasn't there when he announced to all who would listen that the Americans were for real ("they are a very dangerous team"). And I wasn't there when Hemond almost died from the effects of the same ovarian staph infection and internal bleeding that slowed her in Oman. I wasn't even there when Burnett and the SEALs began planning for the 1994 Raid, to be held in Borneo ("The Land of the Headhunters"). It was a race, they all privately agreed, that they would win.

No, by then I was on my way to London, where I stayed in the flat of David and Catherine Walker, two friends of my sister, Monique. They were gone for the weekend. I had the run of the place.

"Having oatmeal and coffee," begins my journal entry for December 4. "The wind rattles the pane next to the pine table where I eat breakfast. Pine: shades of the Hotel Au Transit. I'm jet-lagged, dehydrated, and world weary right now, but yesterday I managed to do the walking tour of London: Buckingham Palace to Big Ben and Westminster Abbey to the Imperial War Museum, then back to Victoria Station. A long way on a brisk day, but what a city. I'm restless, restless.

It's been just two days, but I'm already beginning to appreciate the significance of the Raid. It meant a great deal to me, now that I look back. It was the first time I ever worked without a net, without a support network. No wife, no kids, telephone, warm bed, shower, cooked food, fast food, or day-to-day order. There was no past or future, just the present."

I was sure I would never go back to the Raid. I wandered through it detached and defensive, not connecting with the country or any single person beyond David Tracey, whom I already knew. Still, I believe that everything happens for a reason, and beyond expanding my little world I could think of just one other good reason I made the trip.

The very first day of the Raid I was rearranging my pack on the sandbar at AP1. I was accosted by two Madagascan policemen wearing automatic rifles. Young and surly, decked out in tan uniforms and black berets, they were my worst nightmare of Third World authority figures come to life. I envisioned arrest for no reason, a filthy, overcrowded jail cell, a ten-year sentence without trial. Nothing good can possibly come of this meeting, I thought as they eyed me and my belongings.

"You are here with the Raid Gauloises?" the one to my left asked. He looked no older than seventeen. One finger was curled around the trigger guard of his AK-47. The contents of my backpack were of great interest to him. I assumed he was looking for signs of drugs or illegal contraband.

"Yes, I am."

"And you are American?"

Great. He'd figured out the accent. Visions of flag burning, Uncle Sam hung in effigy, anti-American brutality.

"Uh . . . yeah."

The one on the right hadn't spoken. I noticed he had his eye on a brand new T-shirt I'd gotten at a 10k run. In the spirit of diplomacy and self-preservation, I offered it to him. "I can have this?" He was ambivalent. Major faux pas, I suddenly realized.

He pulled out a small notebook and the stub of a pencil. He handed them to me. "Write your name," he said firmly.

I nervously printed my name. I handed back his notebook. He studied my handwriting, as did his partner. They took turns sounding out my name, trying to sound American. Then the one on the right—the one I'd given the T-shirt to—took his finger off the trigger long enough to reach out and happily shake my hand. "My wife just had a baby," he exclaimed, "and I will name him after you." The two of them clapped me on the back and went on their way, alternately examining the T-shirt and my name, looking somehow cosmopolitan.

And I'm not sure how that very kind policeman broke the news to his wife ("Honey, I'm home. Wait'll you here the name I came up with . . ."), or whether she agreed to go along at all, but the possibility exists that somewhere in central Madagascar is a boy with my name.

I imagine his wardrobe is filled with Michael Jordan T-shirts.

CHAPTER 3

The Temple of Doom

Borneo, 1994

"When you come to a fork in the road, take it."

Yogi Berra

MADAGASCAR WOULD be the last time the number of Raid participants in America could be counted on one hand. Not only did Steines' ESPN documentary elicit a wondrous response (and subsequent phone calls to Burnett, now the Raid's US liaison), but an NBC *Dateline* documentary raised public awareness even higher. People seemed to remember it as the race where people had the awful feet, an image created from several gruesome NBC shots of Team American Pride in transition.

Fueled by this greater awareness, Burnett's vision of holding a Raid-style race in the US came closer and closer to reality. He and Terkelsen scouted locations in Montana and Wyoming. The target date for the big event was September, just a month before the 1994 Raid in Borneo. Instead of Raid Gauloises, Burnett chose the name "Eco-Challenge." It was his belief that corporate America, specifically the major shoe and outdoor apparel companies from whom he hoped to extract the majority of his $1.5 million budget, would respond better to an event with an ecological ring. He pursued this vision with religious zeal, working the phones side by side with Terkelsen in a small office just off his living room. Their efforts weren't in vain: early on the two turned down several hundred thousand dollars from a major shoe company looking to buy their Eco-Challenge concept. With Terkelsen's detailed business plan as proof that potential Eco-Challenge earnings would make a couple hundred thousand look like chump change, they turned that company down (Terkelsen predicted pre-tax profits would rise from $13,799 in 1993 all the way to $2,566,448 in 1997, the last year of the five-year plan). However, since those potential earnings weren't exactly flooding in the door, Burnett and Terkelsen were forced to push the inaugural Eco back to May 1995.

As far as the Raid went, Burnett's plan was to compete one more time, then quit to focus on the business side. The perfect conclusion would be American Pride winning in Borneo. Ensuing publicity would fuel Eco-Challenge fever and help build the persona of swaggering outdoor adventurer that Burnett was fashioning for himself. As a build-up to Borneo he even staged a tryout in May for Susan Hemond's successor, complete with NBC *Dateline* filming the weekend-long proceedings.

Perhaps the best indicator that Raid-style racing had a future in America came in August at the Outdoor Retailer trade show in Reno, the convention where all the hot new outdoor trends get showcased. Eco-Challenge was an exciting new market segment for the outdoor industry, the first event ever to combine a little of everything—from boots to bikes to 'biners—they sold. If the event took off like Burnett and Terkelsen were predicting—and by then Burnett was even saying Eco-Challenge would someday be bigger than any other endurance race in history—the horde of new competitors would equate to vast new market share. Small wonder that the booth for Hi-Tec hiking boots, the company that eventually paid Burnett $500,000 to be Eco's title sponsor, was designed entirely around the Eco-Challenge concept. A film clip starring and narrated by Burnett explaining the Raid/Eco ideal rolled continuously on an overwide screen. Hi-Tec's booth was the talk of the show.

My greatest shock came in the uniform Hi-Tec's employees wore: a khaki carbon copy of the Raid's journalist shirt, but with the Eco logo over the breast pocket. They looked like a bunch of poseurs.

Still, despite the growing awareness and fabricated hype, there was an innocence to everything surrounding Raid-style racing. We all knew each other and each other's spouses. We possessed a fascination with our peculiar, unknown sport. Through regular conversations with Burnett and Terkelsen and the members of American Pride, I found myself more and more immersed in the Raid/Eco culture. As trying as Madagascar had been, witnessing the Raid unfold was so singular that it stayed with me long after I got home. I felt incredibly close to those who had shared the experience. To others, even Calene, it was impossible to explain my growing preoccupation.

In those three pivotal weeks in Madagascar, an unseen umbilical cord between me and the corporate world was snipped nearly in two. The subtle schedules and movements of superiors and coworkers that had always defined my day—had defined me—were left behind, bringing forth a sense of true independence and the sudden belief that I could do anything with my life that I wanted.

Which was good, because Keith fired me my first day back. It was done over lunch, surgically, with a casual tone of British afterthought. It was made to sound like it was in my best interest. And though Keith didn't know it, that actually was true. I needed to leave the corporate world. By staying I risked becoming a poster child for inertia. I only wish I'd had the balls to quit before I was pushed. But that's hindsight. In reality, I needed the security of a regular paycheck. Which is why my first move after lunch wasn't to race from the building and leap headlong into the unstructured world of freelance writing. It was back to my office, where I sent out resumes to occupations smacking of creativity like public relations and advertising, with plans to continue my writing in the morning, before work. After the full-blown independence of the Raid, it was a scheme doomed from the very first interview.

The executive was an unsmiling woman with perfect posture, a navy suit, and brown hair in a professional bun. She had been a journalist once, doing hard news for National Public Radio before switching to the higher-paying world of public relations. She let slip that her hobby was traveling to underdeveloped countries. "Oh, really?" I said, fishing for common ground. Things hadn't been going well. The questions were getting perfunctory. "I just got back from Madagascar."

She eyed me with icy suspicion. "How did you like it?"

"It was different," I babbled happily. "I was hungry all the time. Tell you what, I would have killed for a Taco Bell." She raised an eyebrow primly and folded her hands as if to pray. I got the sensation she was personally responsible for the Third World's public relations. They were her personal domain, a forbidden world she lectured about with authority at cocktail parties.

"I would hate to see a nation like that compromised by capitalism," she snipped.

For the sake of a potential paycheck, I bit my tongue. Maybe Taco Bell isn't the answer, but the Third World needs a solid dose of capitalism or its countries will forever be filled with open sewers, unbridled disease, and peasants with no future. People like my interviewer, I'm sure, would rather they remain that way, for whatever personal conceits. The noble savage isn't as noble as people would like to believe. My guess is he'd rather be the very wealthy savage.

It was a few more interviews before I figured out that personnel at allegedly creative companies were just as button-down, just as stilted, just as corporate and cloistered as those at a rigid engineering firm like the one I had worked for. They might not wear pocket protectors or sleep with calculators, but their work environment was as uptight as if they did. I went home after one particularly bad interview during which my less-than-conservative politics were questioned, then lampooned, ready to spring an idea on Calene that had been bubbling in my head. "I don't want to do this anymore," I began. "I'm a writer. That's what I want to do for a living. Nothing else. And if it's meant to be, then it's meant to be, but I should at least give it a try to find out."

We argued that night and the whole week after. Then one evening I came home to find her staring at a picture on our fridge. It was a goofy shot, me on a white-sand beach in southwestern Madagascar, leaping through the air like Peter Pan with a pen and notebook in my outstretched hands. I was trying to show the photographer a maneuver I sometimes did to amuse my boys.

Calene was studying the shot, looking mostly at my face. "You look so happy there," she said, tapping it with a fingernail. "That's the happiest I've seen you in years."

I'd been ready for another round of battle. The change relaxed me. I stepped closer and examined my image, not saying anything. Calene's not one for speaking in metaphors, so what she said next had the real ring of insight. "It's almost like you're making a leap of faith. Tell me this: Can you support us as a writer?" I've always considered myself a spiritual man, and in her change of heart—hard on the heels of every other amazing incident—I could see the hand of God pushing me in a certain direction, opening all the doors that needed to be opened. It was time to take the leap of faith.

I sold Raid stories to eight magazines. Only two were feature length (the others were just a few paragraphs). But writing them, I came to embrace both my new profession and the Raid itself. In the rear-view mirror, Madagascar wasn't half as bad as I had felt mid-Raid. Dangers and hardships were shrunken by distance and time; personalities remembered only for their good. Antoine was no longer the reluctant administrator, but Yves Montand with a clipboard. David Tracey became the chorus in a Greek tragedy.

Calene's support in the months that followed my leaving the corporate world was the greatest source of inspiration I have ever known. She encouraged me to dream, then make those dreams happen. Her support was unwavering, even when I discovered doubt within myself. When assignments were offered in faraway places like Tokyo and Hawaii, she encouraged me to go and make the most of them. The fire truck, of course, came with me.

So I was ready in September when Graem Sims, deputy editor of one of Australia's biggest sports publications, called from Australia. "I've just seen an Australian Army report about the rivers of Borneo," he said merrily, his voice betraying a certain morbid amusement, "and they have all the makings of being a rather deadly place to get stuck. Apparently, the observer witnessed several carnivorous reptiles lolling about on the banks and in the shallows. In one instance, remarkable actually, the fellow witnessed a very large log—it says here the size of a telephone pole—floating down river. It got sucked into a rather large whirlpool. The force of the whirlpool stood the log on end like a swizzle stick and sucked it under."

Graem paused. He is a thin, serious man, whose taste for adventure is strictly voyeuristic. Graem is comfortable sending others on assignment into the great outdoors, but prefers for himself the comforts of domesticated events like soccer and Aussie Rules Football, where the bar, hot food, and the comforts of home are never far off. Which, when all is said and done, is not exactly senseless.

He cleared his throat dramatically. "The observer kept searching for the log to pop back up, but it never did." Another pause. Sims was milking the moment, setting me up for the grand finale. "So, do you think you'd like to give it a go—cover the Raid Gauloises one more time, mate?"

Well, why not? Borneo would be a magnificent adventure, with far more potential for calamity and catastrophe. Inhabited by head-hunters until World War II, it is an island of nothing but claustrophobic jungle—unpredictable, in-your-face, omnipresent. Crocodiles and sharks, Madagascar's threat, were just the stepping-off point in Borneo's little shop of horrors. There would also be leopards, cobras, and other large poisonous snakes, orangutans, monitor lizards as big as a man, and mosquitoes carrying malaria and dengue fever. There would be bats, as well. Borneo is home to the Mulu caves, the world's largest network of limestone caverns, spanning almost 200 underground miles. They were relevant because spelunking was a new event for 1994, replacing skydiving.

Even Borneo's parasite of choice would be ghastlier and more cunning than Madagascar's. "Wait 'til your hear this," David said, calling a month before we were due to meet in the Malaysian city of Kuching. He would be covering the Japanese teams again. "I was talking with a friend who just got back from Borneo. He says that under no circumstances are you to wade into a river to take a leak. There's a parasite that's attracted to the warmth of the piss. It follows the stream back into your body, swimming all the way up your urethra."

"No shit?"

"No shit. And that's not even the good part. Once it gets inside your member it lodges itself inside the urethra with these barbs that it's got on the outside of its body."

"No shit?"

"No shit. My friend got it. He said that once the thing's lodged inside, the only thing to do is run, not walk, to the doctor and beg for him to cut off your dick."

"No shit?"

"No shit."

I had to go. Borneo is an island whose very name conjures up the primitive and deadly. It's divided among three countries: Malaysia, Indonesia, and Brunei. The Raid would be held in the Malaysian sector, a state known as Sarawak, which covers the upper third of Borneo. It was a British colony until World War II, when the Japanese swept in and made it their own. After the war, when the British Empire splintered, it became independent. Modern Malaysia still speaks English as the national language, but now considers itself a Muslim country and no longer has a European feel. So what used to be a nation of warring headhunters is now filled with either devout Muslims or headhunters turned farmers being told they should be devout Muslims.

Green is the color that springs immediately to mind when I think of Borneo. It's a giant, saturated sponge that will never wring out, segmented by those brown stretches of trouble Sims spoke of, then swaddled in a triple canopy cocoon. It smells like a golf course that's been watered too much. When the rains come and the rivers overflow their banks and the native longboats can barely navigate the current, it becomes more obvious than ever that Borneo is a place where the land tames the people instead of the people taming the land. Samling, the national logging company, is trying to remedy that problem by clear-cutting the jungle, tree by tree. Logging roads—the only roads to be found in the jungle—gash from sea to interior, a capillary network no less obvious or obscene than the red veins striping the nose of a lifelong drunk. "We are only cutting down old trees," a government official would tell me one typically hot, muggy afternoon.

"Then why are there no trees?" I said, looking out over a swath of jungle laid bare. Mile after mile of clear-cut denudement spread before us.

"They were all old."

Besides the assignment, a major reason for going to Borneo was Team American Pride. I believed that the talent and professionalism of the SEALs would help them become the first American team to win, and I wanted to see them stomp the French in person. A touchy personnel-chemistry problem from Madagascar had been resolved when Susan Hemond, told by doctors that she risked death by competing again, announced her retirement. It was obviously time for her to go.

Hemond's replacement was Cathy Sassin-Smith, a bodybuilder and nutritionist from Santa Monica who was chosen through a tryout in the mountains above Burnett's Los Angeles home. For three days and nights, fifteen women simulated a mini-Raid under the guidance of the SEALs. Forced marches, midnight paddling in the nearby ocean, sleep and food deprivation. In short, cold, wet, tired, hungry, and miserable combined with Harwood's SEAL-learned penchant for mind games.

"Now that might be a pleasant walk in the daytime," he pointed out to me the first night of the tryout. We were standing on a bridge over-looking swampy Topanga Creek at midnight. The night air was cold and damp enough to make me shiver in a fleece jacket. The women had just walked under the bridge, to follow the creek five miles to the ocean. "The sun's on your back, there's a little water on your feet, some pretty trees . . . But at night it's different. At night it's black. You can't see where you're going. You don't know whether that thing rubbing against your leg is a branch or a snake. At night, your fears take over, and this is about conquering your fears."

Sassin-Smith's victory was not popular. The other women felt she was chosen through the influence of her employer, Gold's Gym, which also happened to be a financial backer of Team American Pride. That wasn't the case. Team American Pride, including Hemond, cast the final votes. To them it was obvious that Sassin-Smith possessed the characteristics of the best Raiders: an easy smile, comfort within a team setting, outstanding physical fitness, and a desire to finish at all costs.

The fact that just one team from America would race the Raid made the tryout all the more special. In effect, of all the women in America, only one—the one chosen at Team American Pride's tryout—would be allowed to compete in Borneo. So when Sassin-Smith was selected four months before the Raid's October 17 start, that seemed a likely end to the story for the other tryout participants.

But it wasn't. In a move that saw the first-ever moments of disharmony among American Raid followers, a group of the women combined to form a team of their own. They went around Burnett and contacted Fusil personally in order to secure entry. They called themselves Team American Pride–Woman. Though they wouldn't be the first all-female team at the Raid (W' OMAN, a group of French women had the honor in Oman and Madagascar), the five would be the first American team of the sort. As a result of their bitter tryout experience and Burnett's attempts to prevent them from competing, their disregard toward both Burnett and the other members of Team American Pride bordered on the adversarial. By October, neither team was speaking to the other.

Which may or may not explain why the women arrived for the prologue race in the coastal city of Kuching with a monstrous American flag in tow, literally duplicating the symbolic flag-waving that led the French to loathe the men's squad in Oman and Madagascar. The flag was taller even than the women themselves, so huge that it dragged on the ground. And while they did it to establish some legitimacy—shouting to the world that they too represented America—the garish display only succeeded in replacing whatever sympathies the French might have had for an all-women's team with outright disdain.

During the prologue, which was 400 miles from the actual Raid course, and designed to determine starting position (jungle trails on the Raid course would be so narrow that teams would have to travel single file, making a mass start out of the question), the women got so lost that jungle guides were sent in to find them. They would start the Raid in last place.

The prerace briefing was the next day. Fusil, as always, introduced each team. When Team American Pride–Woman was announced, there was weak applause, a collective titter, then a groundswell chant from every French team in the room. "Where's your flag? Where's your flag? Where's your flag?" Mocking and scornful, there was no trace of humor in the collective taunt. Team American Pride–Woman were shamed into keeping their mouths shut—and flag tucked away—for the Raid's duration.

Americans, for some odd reason, could do no right at the Raid Gauloises. It was like a curse.

I was in the center of the room, scrunched next to David and a gaggle of other journalists, awash in the nuance of the spectacle: the mingling of French and English accents, the prerace tension, the taut feeling of competitive juices waiting to be unleashed. I had been an outcast of my own choosing in Madagascar. But I felt like an insider in Borneo. It was good to see Gerard again, wearing his omnipresent walkie-talkie shoulder holster. And Antoine, heavy-lidded from late hours, still smoking Gitanes. Fanny and the fashion models were back, too. Equatorial heat and humidity somehow felt like a cleansing sauna. Even the jungle, which surrounded the picture windows of our meeting room, look inviting instead of threatening. The expectation of adventure thrilled me and I was surprisingly glad to be back at the Raid.

Fusil launched into a summary of the course. Teams followed along on their brand-new maps. The order of events: jungle orienteering, whitewater canoeing, whitewater rafting, mountain biking, spelunking, then more canoeing. In keeping with Fusil's belief that the Raid should be in harmony with the host country, it would be a water-oriented race. The paddling legs would take place on two primary rivers, the Tutoh and the Kubaan. At peak strength they were capable of bringing the swizzle stick scenario to life, substituting hapless competitors for telephone poles. They were muddy rivers, Fusil pointed out, muddy and fast, filled with all manner of wildlife. "The level of the river water is very important," he warned. "If the rivers are high, they will be very dangerous. The current will be almost uncontrollable." He didn't mention how lethargic and easily navigable the rivers became if lack of rainfall forced them to drop even two or three feet, which was important because the equatorial October had been exceedingly dry so far.

Before the rivers there would be 100 miles of jungle trekking. Starting in the remote Christian mission outpost of Ba Kelalan, so far inland that the Indonesian border was just a valley away, teams would follow a tangled network of native hunting trails up over a 9,000-foot summit known as Gunung Murud. Then they would descend through bamboo forests to the water. The course would pass through Long Semeran, a former headhunters' village, and Bareo, home of the resistance movement against the Japanese in World War II (a soccer pitch built by British soldiers was still in use by local children).

"There is jungle everywhere," Fusil cautioned. "Take care. It will be very hard to find your way if you get lost. Be conscious that you are on your own. Be careful where you walk. Stay together all the time because in a few meters you can get lost. This year, more than other years, you must think of the Raid Gauloises as an expedition."

He went into great detail about leeches, the jungle's ubiquitous parasite. They latched onto clothing then worked their way insidiously

to the skin, where they burrowed in and drank of the host's blood, growing quickly from the size of an apostrophe on the printed page to three
bloated inches long. Removing leeches meant a lighter or cigarette to
burn them off, otherwise the head stayed inside the skin to leave a horrible black and blue scar. Teams would talk about leeches well after the
race ended, how they wriggled under thick socks, into underwear, onto
testicles, down backs. Leech stories became as common at the Borneo
Raid as fish stories at a Montana trout stream.

Jungle undergrowth isn't conducive to landing strips, so the
logistics of hauling the Raid expeditionary force from our luxury hotel
on the beach in Kuching across the width of the entire state of Sarawak
to the starting line meant more than just piling everyone aboard a DC-3.
Rather, it would take the better part of a day and require five different
modes of mostly uncommon transportation.

The Raid was due to begin at noon on Monday, October 17. At 1 AM
on the sixteenth, just long enough after the briefing to eat and grab a
last shower in our rooms at the Kuching Holiday Inn, we began our
trek. The easy part was first, the requisite minibuses of gear and racers
motoring sixty miles in caravan to the Kuching Airport. After that,
Antoine wouldn't tell anyone the travel itinerary. "I cannot tell you what
is to come," he said with calm, knowing distance, "it would ruin the
wonderful adventure that lies before you."

"You mean there's more to come after this flight?"

"Oui." He spoke it like a Parisian, even though he is a Parisian by way
of New Caledonia. It came out sounding like "way" instead of "wee."
"Oh, much, much more."

David was behind me in line, reading a book of Tolstoy's short stories while standing up. "I don't like the sound of that," he murmured.
"When Antoine gets that fiendish tone in his voice, it means we're in
for a long day."

We were. From Kuching we flew by light aircraft to Labuan,
a dot of an island off the north coast of Borneo. Labuan is a commercial
hub in Asia due to its large natural harbor and lack of tariffs. Pink clouds
of dawn replaced night outside my window as we angled in to land. I
scanned Labuan through the small porthole. By all appearances it was
an unremarkable claptrap of an island, filled from one end to the other

with rundown apartment buildings and back alley bazaars. Enormous tankers and cargo ships lay just off the coast. We shuttled the five-minute drive from the airport to the harbor, then unloaded in front of what looked like a Greyhound bus station. Small lobby, plastic chairs, vending machines, linoleum floors, vacant ticket counter. Three hundred of us crowded inside, tossing packs on the floor and against the walls, trying to snatch sleep as we awaited the next leg.

"What now?" I said to Antoine. He was talking to Fanny. His eyebrows were arched. Someone told me once that they used to be an item. I gathered Antoine was laying the groundwork for a jungle reunion.

"Express boat," he said, not taking his eyes from Fanny.

"What's an express boat?"

"You will see."

"Why can't you just tell me?" I felt like a pest.

"Because I cannot. It would ruin the adventure."

Antoine and I had an understanding. I would ask too many questions of him and he, in turn, would shrug and puff on his cigarette several times and roll his eyes before not sharing the answer. It was the nature of things, a game. Sometimes when I desperately needed to know an important piece of information, I would try reverse psychology and ask the question rhetorically, as if my taunting assumption that the question would go unanswered might lead him to tell me out of unbridled Gallic pride. Sometimes, when my timing was just right and my tone suitably skeptical, it worked.

But even that ploy couldn't get him to tell me about express boats. It was up to David, who also played the Antoine game, to clue me in. "Express boats are a fuselage without wings. They're suicide machines. You get inside, and if it sinks you go down because there's no way out. You've never been on one?"

"I never even heard the term until ten minutes ago."

"Oh, you'll like it. They're all over Asia because they get lots of people to where they want to go in a hurry. They're a kick." He went back to Tolstoy.

The two express boats that would carry the Raiders from Labuan back to the Bornean mainland arrived presently, pulling into the dock behind the Waterworld bus station. They were indeed fuselage without wings; porthole-lined tubes with a hull, driven by massive unmuffled engines in the rear. A throaty basso rumble and the smell of diesel filled the air as they maneuvered into their slips. The drivers were dressed like working men instead of ships' captains; Teamsters, plying a different sort of highway.

The Raiders piled aboard, single file. The cabin was the spitting image of an airliner's, with rows of three seats on either side of a single aisle. A bootleg copy of Arnold Schwarzenegger's *True Lies*, which hadn't been released on video in America, played on a monitor near the entrance. The aroma of mothballs and undiluted insecticide permeated the small space. Several people already wore bandannas covering their mouths. The runner in me doubted the wisdom of breathing that air for any length of time, even with a bandanna. I schemed for a minute, looking for options. On the way in I had noticed a small deck outside on the bow, just in front of the captain's canopy. Figuring that it was better to seek forgiveness than ask permission, I grabbed my pack and meandered back up top into fresh air. The boat was backing out already, rumbling for the South China Sea. Five Raiders were up top ahead of me.

By the time we reached the mainland two hours later, there wasn't a single person left below. Driven out by the smell, competitors and journalists crowded the small foredeck. Many had even clambered onto the curved top of the fuselage. I spent most of the journey balancing atop the curve myself, trying to ignore the obvious peril. The sun had come up low and slow, backlighting freighters and tankers waddling through the tranquil straits. With a bit of balance and flexibility I could lie back and watch the clouds turn from pink to yellow to white as the sun rose higher in the sky. All in all, it was a wonderful journey.

We approached, then passed, the coast of Borneo without stopping. We motored at full speed up a wide river for two more hours, throwing a fierce wake that swamped the thick reeds in the shallows, then overflowed into the jungle behind. There was a giddy silence about the boat as we moved upstream. It was the first time most of us had seen true jungle. As Markman noted in Costa Rica, there's an amazing resemblance to the Jungle Cruise at Disneyland, from the thick mixture of bamboo rods and tall, leafy trees on down to the greenish-brown river water. We studied it with amazement, searching for signs of wildlife. A wave of humidity carried the complex smell of rot and decay and constant rebirth to us. Despite the Disney similarity, it all appeared very forbidding and intimidating. I imagined thousands of hidden predatorial eyes looking back at us. My one overwhelming thought was that if I walked through there alone I would surely perish.

We finally moored in a dusty, backwater river port. Barefoot locals eyed us. They looked like river pirates, with their tattered clothes and hooded glances. "What next?" I asked Antoine.

"You will ride in trucks."

Disney time again. I live just minutes from Disneyland. Calene and I even own those annual passports, which means unlimited year-round entrance. The best time to go is in spring and fall (the off-season) when the tourists are home in Iowa or Iraq or wherever else it is they've flown in from. The rides have ridiculously short lines, and it's possible to zoom through Splash Mountain and Star Tours and Thunder Mountain Railroad several times in a day. That's unheard of in the middle of summer, when the wait for each ride can often stretch to over two hours.

It's a fairy tale world, to be sure, waltzing in and out of Disneyland's altered reality whenever the whim strikes. But it's an adventure unto itself. And if it was possible for the theme park to imitate the jungle, as in the case of the river passage, why couldn't the jungle imitate the theme park? Like I was boarding a Disney ride, I took my cue from Antoine and climbed in back of one of the seventy-five four-wheel-drive pickup trucks lined up quayside. A Bornean driver rode up front. Passengers rode in the bed, unencumbered by eccentricities like seat belts.

My truck had three other American journalists inside. There was Sean Arbabi, a photographer with a boyish face and absurd sense of humor. Mark Steines was doing another Raid documentary. Trent Kamerman was the final guy on board. Kamerman was Steines' camera man. Tall, with a wonderfully dopey grin, Trent was newly married. He had arrived home from his honeymoon just two days before leaving for the Raid and would spend his entire time in Borneo mooning over pictures of his new bride. It would have been comically sappy if it hadn't reminded me so much of how I'd behaved in Madagascar. Poor Trent, the day after returning from Borneo he got a call asking him to fly to Russia to film hockey players for ESPN. (Trent collapsed on that trip, the result of an insect bite in the Bornean jungle. He almost died when the Russian doctors—knowing more about frostbite than obscure tropical diseases—couldn't diagnose his mystery illness for several days.)

The first hour was easy, a gentle drive along surprisingly pastoral local roads. The overgrown green countryside looked like Wisconsin gone to seed. We didn't talk much, just watched the jungle roar past in a sixty-mph blur. I thought of napping.

Then things changed.

I don't remember ever looking at our driver. I don't remember actually glimpsing the face of the man that scared the living daylights out of us for the next three hours, a man seemingly born with an unquenchable desire for thrill seeking and the delusion that he was Borneo's answer to Junior Johnson. For as soon as we made a casual left turn onto a wide, muddy Samling logging road, he drove that little pickup to the very outside of the envelope. Hour after hour we pitched up and down those muddy, mountainous roads. Steep, mile-long downhills were handled without brakes, in a state of near freefall. Uphills were an excuse to ride with two wheels hanging off the shoulder. The hairpin turns—and every turn was a hairpin—were taken at full speed, the back end sliding in and out of control in the muddy slop. It was like riding a roller-coaster without a track, always sure that the very next turn was the one that would launch us into space. We whooped and hollered and hung on for dear life accordingly. Given that all this took place inside one of the world's last unexplored jungles, the ride felt overwhelmingly surreal. Disney-ish, even.

We stopped halfway to refuel, filling our tanks at a pyramid of fifty-five-gallon fuel drums in a clear-cut section of jungle. We parked in bright yellow mud six inches deep. A layer of gasoline coated the earth in vast puddles. The same foul mixture coated our boots when we stepped down to stretch our legs.

"Marty?" It was Sean, looking at what gasoline and yellow mud had done to his brand new pair of boots.

"Yeah?"

"Try not to step in the mud." The sentence would become Sean's Borneo calling card, an ironic poke at the filth we walked in, slept in, and ate in. *Mud* and *Borneo* will forever be synonymous in my mind, much more so than *Borneo* and *Jungle*, or *Borneo* and *Danger*.

The trip ended another hour later, at yet another logging camp. The mud was even thicker and stronger, capable of sucking a foot in and holding it. Walking was laborious and precarious, especially with a full pack. "Alo, Martin," Antoine called as I began looking for high ground. I meant to take a peek at our driver, but he'd already gone back, trying to make it to his version of civilization before sunset.

"Antoine, my good friend who never answers questions. What's next?"

"Oh . . . you will be very happy. We just walk," and here he used two fingers to simulate a walking motion, "and then you will be at the starting line in Ba Kelalan."

"How far's the walk?"

"You will see." He pointed to the jungle. "The trail is that way."

Rain began to fall as we ambled through the jungle muck. It was my first time actually walking inside a jungle, and I found it surprisingly tranquil. The sensation was more like a dense forest than anything else. Initial fears set aside, I began to look forward to the hike ahead.

We marched close together, in groups of ten or twenty, careful not to stray from the trail into the wall of green that surrounded us. The trail was thin and shaped like a culvert from all the rain, so much so that it was easier to walk straddling the trail than in the center of the trail itself. A poncho kept my head dry, but did nothing for my feet when water filled the trail. The poncho also did little to protect my legs and rear end when I slipped on the slick jungle leaves and mud. Or when I splashed down into the middle of the moving trail, where I would slide several feet before self-arresting on a root or low tree branch. We all took turns falling. I certainly didn't expect to make it through the Raid without getting thoroughly soaked and filthy, but I was surprised it had happened so quickly.

Finally, eighteen wet and wild hours after leaving Kuching, we stepped from the trees into Ba Kelalan, a tranquil, thousand-acre oasis covered with rice paddies. There was also a school and a church, and even a native choir that would serenade us that night at the pre-race ceremony. I paused as we came into the valley, letting my pack straps slip off my shoulders. That I was up to my ankles in a puddle didn't concern me, for the sensation of water-filled shoes had long ago ceased being uncomfortable.

"Marty?" Sean said, stopping next to me.

"Yeah?"

"Try not to step in the mud."

A few days later the same group of us sat around a table, swatting mosquitoes and telling jokes. "How are you going to call this sport in your stories?" Steines asked me. "With the Eco-Challenge coming to America we can't call it the Raid anymore."

"What are you going to call it?"

"I was thinking of expedition racing. Or maybe nature racing."

"Those are pretty good." The table grew silent.

"There's a name I've been toying with for awhile," I said after a minute. The name was one I'd used in a pre-Raid piece in the October *Competitor.* On deadline, stuck for a term to define the sport, I'd written the first one that came to mind. "How about adventure racing? I think I'll try that one for awhile and see if it sticks."

Amazingly, it did.

THE RAID began the next day at noon exactly. The reasons Team American Pride got lost immediately are many, but focus mainly around lack of communication within their edgy, fractured unit and the dogged belief that they were the team most capable of winning. While others simply marched to the edge of Ba Kelalan, took a left turn at the large, steaming water buffalo patty, then followed a hunting trail to the first checkpoint atop Gunung Murud, American Pride thought that too obvious. Instead, they tried to clear a path using machetes.

But the jungle was so claustrophobic that just five feet of forward motion took ten minutes of whacking. At that rate it would have taken days to march the six miles to the mountain top. To make matters worse, the terrain wasn't a simple incline, but sharp waves of cliffs and deep valleys. More than once Team American Pride built up a head of steam, only to find themselves atop a cliff for which they had no ropes to descend. Frustrated, they would backtrack hours in another direction, rerouting on the fly. "We always knew where we were," Holman said later, pointing to a sweat-stained topographical map, "but we just didn't know how to get where we needed to be."

Once the frustration of being lost evolved into the realization that teams like Jura and Malaysia's own Team Samling were two, then four, then eight hours ahead, Burnett added insult to injury by talking of quitting. Since Raid rules stipulate that unless the entire team finishes, the squad is disqualified, Burnett's quitting would remove Team American Pride from the race, even if all the others finished. "We have absolutely no reason to finish," he told the team. "I don't need to be kicked in the shins to know it hurts."

I had helicoptered to the top of Gunung Murud to wait for them. At 9,000 feet, the summit was bitterly cold and damp, the kind that settles into your bones, impervious to layered jackets and hot coffee. The contrast was especially sharp after Ba Kelalan, where constant rain and equatorial heat made for a thick steam bath between showers. The mud on Gunung Murud was coal black instead of yellow. An errant Antarctic wind gusted so fiercely that the helicopter pilots practiced the most focused sort of professionalism with every landing and takeoff. Normally chatty and nonchalant, they would cease all talk and focus on the circle of trees surrounding the narrow helipad, which was merely a pair of lumber pallets arranged atop the mud. Their unspoken fear was obvious to all passengers: A slight miscalculation or subtle wind shift and the rotors would slam hard into the trees and send us careening helplessly across the landscape. Nobody wants to die, especially not a grisly death in such a bleak place.

Gunung Murud was unusual for more reasons than just cold and winds. The missionaries at Ba Kelalan, who practice a charismatic form of Roman Catholicism, decided in the late 1980s that God was calling them to build a sacred place of worship, a church to be used only on Easter and Christmas. That place, they decided through prayer and soul-searching, was atop Gunung Murud. With that settled, the entire populace of Ba Kelalan hiked to the summit over the very same trail being followed by the Raiders. They built an enormous red church and a network of traditional Bornean longhouses to provide sleeping and eating areas. Lumber sidewalks linked the society. Outhouses were built in traditional native fashion—with the seat hovering over a stream. And while the term "flush toilet" took on new meaning, I never again drank from a Bornean creek, no matter how sparkling the water appeared.

At nightfall I sat cross-legged on the covered patio of a longhouse, wrapped in a fleece pullover and poncho as hard rain pelted Gunung Murud. I was sure that American Pride would be one of the first teams, as a quick look at the course had convinced me that winning tactics wouldn't allow for the patience Jura exhibited in Madagascar. The winning team in Borneo would be the team that made it to the rivers first. Paddling would be the toughest leg, but the fastest as well. And because the mountain biking leg was just thirty miles and the caving twenty, there would be little in the way of grueling distance for teams to make up a deficit after the rivers.

So I waited with great anticipation, not knowing that Team American Pride was hopelessly lost. The other English-speaking journalists waited close by. Sean played with his lenses, fussing over the flat light. Mark and Trent looked for the most dramatic place to shoot the leader's arrival, finally deciding it would be best if they actually got out into the downpour for that "you are there" feel. David and I debated idly on the covered patio, about authors and religion and the source of the droplets of rain plunking off the wooden awning.

Finally, at 5:30, just before dusk, when conversation was running low, a team trotted up the wooden sidewalk. It was Samling, the group sponsored by the Malaysian national logging concern. It included three locals, all cave guides, and two New Zealanders. Oblivious to the cold, they traveled in running shoes, shorts, and T-shirts. They carried microscopic backpacks, with just enough food and water to sustain themselves for the two days it would take them to get to the river. "Traveling light," enthused John Howard, the bearded Kiwi leading them. He was in his early forties and was gaunt enough that people made POW jokes behind his back. "Got to get to the river quickly." Moving quickly out of sight, he recounted that they would have made the summit earlier if a belligerent orangutan hadn't blocked the trail for a half hour.

We continued our wait. Other teams passed through in the next several hours, none of them American Pride. I finally gave up the ghost at midnight, crawling off to sleep in a longhouse still smoky from the evening's cooking fires. Stretched out in my sleeping bag on the bumpy wooden floor, I tossed and turned, waiting for the sound of footfalls on the walkway, wondering again and again about whatever curse it was that prevented Americans from racing successfully at the Raid. I heard the women's team come in, but decided that wasn't the story I was chasing and went back to sleep. Through it all, there was something bothering me—nagging at me—that I couldn't put my finger on. When a team came through at 4 AM I found myself unable to fall back to sleep. I stared up at the low-beamed ceiling and tried to plumb the source of my unsettling thoughts.

First, I admitted to myself what I'd been suppressing since the women's tryout four months before: I was slowly becoming interested in racing the Raid. Where I once saw Raiders as mental and physical supermen, my opinion had changed. Watching the women—all of whom had great heart and incredible stamina but weren't athletes on a remotely Olympian scale—endeavor to become Raiders convinced me that the race was accessible to anyone with enough dedication.

But what was the point? I had nothing to prove. I liked the soft parallel adventure the journalists received compared to the harsher realities of being a competitor. And though I made a painfully honest evaluation of my psyche in search of this sudden motivation, I could think of no earthly reason I should do the Raid other than the inexorable pull of curiosity. I was dedicated to my family and my work, sure the Raid had no relevance in my routine other than as an annual free trip abroad.

I also admitted something more troubling: I had ceased to possess journalistic objectivity. I was openly rooting for American Pride to win, and it concerned me. I like professional distance. It's better to write truthfully and objectively about people from a few paces back. Get too close and views soften. Otherwise thoughtful criticism receives a mental edit. Telling conversations go unwritten. Instead of taking pride in the fact that writing is, of itself, an honorable endeavor, the writer becomes a groupie, a lap dog, a secretary—content to record the acts of others and wallow in hero worship.

I willed myself to sleep by resolving to take two steps back from the American Pride booster club. I chose to ignore my desire to do the Raid, sure that midrace hoopla drove it.

American Pride still hadn't arrived when I woke up two hours later.

I drank my morning coffee over the cooking fire inside the longhouse, then choppered down to Ba Kelalan. Taking one step backward in order to move two steps forward, I hoped to find a ride to Bareo, which was halfway to the Kubaan River. Teams would pass through there by nightfall.

I threw my pack off the chopper first, then stepped out into the wonderfully oppressive warmth. Before me lay a shocking sight: Team American Pride. They had given up their futile thwacking and backtracked to Ba Kelalan to start all over again. Unshaven, exhausted, with jungle filth covering their clothing and hands, the five looked thoroughly ashamed. They didn't see me as I watched them restart their journey, which was fine with me. It was the saddest, most humbling sight I have ever witnessed at the Raid.

There was a runway in Ba Kelalan, one of those really short grass strips built just for small planes. So I wasn't surprised when a pair of ten-passenger Malaysian Air prop planes circled the valley, then dropped out of the sky. They used so little of the airstrip they appeared to have been stopped by an unseen arresting hook.

There were two groups waiting for a flight to Bareo: journalists and Raid dignitaries. The journo plane was first to land, but filled up before I could get aboard. Not knowing better, and unable to understand urgent French exhortations to deplane for some reason or other, I threw my pack in the dignitaries' plane, found a seat, and lost myself in a book. There was a buzz of expectancy in the small craft as it lifted abruptly from Ba Kelalan, climbing steeply to avoid clipping Gunung Murud. I paid no attention, sure that it was typical French fussing and probably related to something culinary or needlessly officious.

Bareo was just a fifteen-minute flight. We circled before landing. From the air I could see that it was another village like Ba Kelalan, a natural clearing surrounded by nothing but jungle. Wispy clouds settled low in the green hills, giving Bareo an almost ethereal spookiness. We landed. Taxied. Came to a halt next to a row of longhouses. I was closest to the door, so when it opened I absentmindedly slung my pack over a shoulder and prepared to deplane. "Non, non," a polite young woman informed me, intimating that I should wait for my more important French friends to deplane first.

One by one they filed out, until at last I was given a nod and a smile from Miss Manners. For some reason that I couldn't understand, she was motioning for me to leave my pack on board—which we both knew to be a serious violation of Raid protocol and basic tenets of self-preservation. I demurred and hoisted my black-and-purple climber's pack onto my right shoulder once again, then ducked to avoid banging my head on the top of the small door as I stepped out.

For the second time in two hours, I exited an aircraft to a shocking sight.

On the grass tarmac, arranged abreast in a single precise line, was a regal welcoming party of forty village elders, male and female. They smiled and shuffled nervously on their feet, preparing to honor their prestigious visitors from the outside world. I got the feeling they'd practiced a few times. The women wore brightly colored robes and had their hair pulled back. Their earrings were heavy brass, making such enormous holes in the lobes that flaps of skin dangled onto their shoulders like long locks of hair. The men wore a mixture of feathered ceremonial headdress and western attire—long khaki pants and lightweight blue sports coats, leather shoes. They stood proudly at attention. Many wore medals given them by the British for their role in the resistance during World War II. Behind them stood just about every noncompetitive member of the Raid party.

A head of state could not have received a more regal greeting. Zelig-like, I had somehow stumbled into the center of the procession. A young local girl—beautiful, black hair, perfect smile—gently took me by the arm and guided me to the receiving line. Someone relieved me of my backpack and I was too overwhelmed to protest. My journalist friends watched in amusement as the locals clamored to show their respect. I played up my new role, stiffening my posture and waving to the journos in that anonymous, vacuous way politicians address their public.

There were ten of us. We lined up facing the villagers. Native girls brought forth a ceremonial juice drink. I could taste pineapple as a hint of fermentation made my tongue numb and mind buzz in the midday sun. Gerard Sepau, owner of Marenco, the production company that films the Raid each year, led the way down the receiving line. I was last, the lone American and English-speaker, shaking hands with my new friends and receiving warm words of welcome. A voice from the crowd—David's—yelled, "Impostor!" I looked for him, but found Antoine instead, rolling his eyes at my sudden importance.

"Salud, salud," he howled. "Salud, king of Borneo!"

My first impulse was to clown, but the dignitaries were so genuinely effusive that it was impossible to downplay the wonder of the moment. I shook each hand and looked into each eye, wondering what stories of true death-defying adventure these people—whose lives had witnessed the era of headhunters, Japanese occupation, and the theft of their jungle by Samling—could tell if pressed. They wouldn't speak on the record, of course—there were rumors that governmental retribution for candid comments could be severe—but I still wanted to hear firsthand their life stories.

But when all was said and done, when the bubble burst and I became just another sweat-soaked journalist, they were nowhere to be found. They were back working their farms, I was told. The floral dresses, brass earrings, and medal-festooned jackets were already back in a trunk someplace, their owners up to their ankles in rice paddy.

I did get plenty of chances to mingle with other locals in Bareo, however. I slept in a longhouse, the traditional communal dwelling, which is raised on stilts and sleeps about a hundred. There was a small restaurant in Bareo, as well. A rice and vegetable dinner cost about three dollars. They sold cold beer and soft drinks too, as Bareo has electricity. All in all, it was like Small Town, USA: a main street, one restaurant, a common-sense local attitude, farming-oriented. I was shocked to find such a place in the middle of a country whose very name is synonymous with "primitive." It was unnerving. I'd come to the Raid for a taste of the raw adventure I'd known in Madagascar. Where was the adventure in sleeping indoors—albeit in a longhouse—eating hot meals and reclining on Main Street with a cold beer after I'd knocked off for the day?

I choppered out after two days to a remote checkpoint, in search of the real Borneo, flying to a logging camp on the Kubaan River, a clear-cut plain of mud where the rafting ended and the mountain biking began. The locals there—filthy, jaded, toothless pirates—ran a mid-jungle trading post that sold hot meals and *Playboy* to logging truck drivers. I wandered down to the Kubaan for my first glimpse of its raw fury, but lack of rain had lowered it six feet. I took a swim in its waters as it meandered slowly, pathetically. No swizzle sticks. No cobras or carnivorous reptiles. For all I knew, no parasites. (Exactly one month later, monsoons slammed into Borneo. The Kubaan raged again.) The Raid has always been subject to the vagaries of local conditions (indeed, race rules allow for sudden course changes based on weather and its effect on the competition. This happens at least once per Raid).

A bust. Not that those didn't exist, but it was obvious there were limits to experiencing them firsthand if I didn't actually get out and whack through the jungle like the competitors.

I pitched my tent on the edge of the clearing. I made a small fire, cooked rice and beans for dinner, then went to bed as the sun went down. It was my token homage to the discipline of simplicity, and seemed out of place amid the logging camp's soft-core raunch.

I caught the first chopper to Mulu the next morning, site of both legendary caves and the finish line. It was Friday, the fifth day of the Raid. It would also be the last. Samling, the team made up of three Malaysian cave guides and two New Zealand endurance athletes, took advantage of the low rivers. Instead of doing battle for days on end—which would have been a handicap, as their Malaysian members had never done technical rafting before—they floated and paddled their way to victory. "Looks like we took your Raid and shortened it," John Howard chortled to Fusil in reference to the blitzkrieg. No Raid had been finished in four and a half days before. What was all the more remarkable was how Samling competed: Wearing running shorts instead of long tights, carrying packs that contained almost no food (and weighed just ten pounds), and without stopping longer than five minutes at transition areas. After Borneo, all competitive Raid teams would race like Samling. Packs would be stripped in a similar manner. The hour-long wine and cigarette breaks between stages would cease.

Meanwhile, waiting for others to finish, I hooked up with Mark and Trent to follow the slow progress of Team American Pride. Each day they'd helicopter into the jungle to film American Pride. Each day I'd watch the rough footage with them when they returned.

The going was slow because the motivation to race all-out had disappeared into a mud of depression after the first day. Team morale was at an all-time low. Burnett had tried to quit often, once going so far as to notify an official at CP4. That's fine, he was told, but the vegetation is too thick to land a helicopter here. If you want to quit you must walk to the next checkpoint. Burnett rescinded his resignation and pushed on. "I was in the best shape of my life," he would say later. "But the mental wear and tear of trying to put together a team for the Raid and coordinate my own race wore me down before I even left for Borneo. I learned a hard lesson that when you do a race like this you must be 100 percent mentally prepared. That means so much more than just physical fitness in terms of getting to the finish line. If you're not mentally fresh, there's no way you can finish."

But it wasn't Burnett who forced American Pride from the race. Team scout Schliemann aggravated a chronic tendon injury by torquing his knee three separate times on slick rocks. When it was finally swollen the size of a grapefruit and he could barely walk, Schliemann allowed the team to call in a rescue helicopter. He refused to look anyone in the eye as he stepped aboard. His unshaven face bore an equally weary and devastated appearance.

With Team American Pride now a nonentity, Burnett dropped out a day later.

I hung around Mulu for five days after Samling finished, waiting for the flight that would take me to the coastal city of Miri, then on to Kuala Lumpur, Taiwan, and Los Angeles. I hiked alone through the jungle to view the awesome Mulu Caves, so tall inside that promotional literature claimed "six 747s can be stacked on top of each other." It was an awesome sight, the inner caverns cool and immense and filled with the sound of unseen running water. The smell of bat guano was overpowering, a heavy, ripe ammonia that leapt right through my nostrils to the core of my brain. At dusk, literally millions of bats flew out the cave mouths and went hunting for bugs. I saw a skull inside the caves, too. It was definitely human, though I tried to tell myself otherwise. Alone in the middle of a remote jungle cavern is not the best time to acknowledge that predators are everywhere.

But I spent most of my time at the finish line, watching teams arrive. There was a ritual to the moment, wherein Fusil would be summoned via walkie-talkie to come welcome the newest group to complete his race. Fusil carried his radio in a black shoulder holster that he wore constantly, so no matter whether the middle of the day or night, he was out there offering congratulations. Fusil greeted each team as if they'd won, squirting them with champagne or Coca-Cola and enduring their sweaty hugs. The women got kisses from Gerard; the men, stolid handshakes, unless they were French and received a kiss on each cheek. That's the way it was when the remnants of American Pride limped in, a disappointing twenty-fifth place. And that's the way it was when Team American Pride–Woman finished, dead last. But my favorite team of all was the one Sims asked me to keep an eye on, Team Australia, led by navigator Bill Proctor and volatile team leader Russell Davis.

Passing through the early checkpoints, they kept within several hours of the leaders. As an hour means very little at the Raid, they weren't concerned about the distance. The more important thing was to keep moving, keep rest to a minimum and avoid those aching emotional lows brought on by lack of sleep that can lead a team to splinter. "I know it sounds corny, mate," Davis confessed to me later, "but when we got to the point where we really felt low," and his voice swooped low on "really" for emphasis, "we'd sing 'Waltzing Matilda'—both the regular and Queensland versions. Like I say, it's corny. But when times are tough, you always go back to where you came from for inspiration."

They sang first on Gunung Murud, where the air was thin and cold and the ground was black mud. They sang it on the shale descending toward Long Rapung, where the bamboo forest grows thick; then again before Bareo, where the road is easy but they'd been walking so many hours that their pack straps dug into their shoulders like hot metal bars and their feet felt sore enough to fall right off their bodies.

Then the Spirit of the Raid reared its enigmatic head. The rain, which had been a source of relentless misery when Team Australia was marching through the jungle, suddenly stopped. The impressionable Tutoh River dropped three feet in as many hours. Team Australia found itself in a low morass, complete with protruding rocks and snagging branches. So Davis and teammate Karen Fry weren't really surprised when their canoe tore a hole. And they weren't really surprised when no way could be found to fix it. What did surprise them was the way they somehow managed to paddle the ragged, impotent craft through the final endless kilometers of Tutoh bump-and-grind. "We ran over so many rocks. It would be paddle, paddle, paddle . . . lift up. And I'd have to lift up or a rock would jam me up the ass," Davis remembered painfully, bouncing up as he spoke for emphasis.

By the time Team Australia finished the canoe leg in the partially deflated boat they had slipped to twentieth position. Teams they had passed days earlier were now in front of them. But they went on. And sang. Both versions. "The mountain bike was bloody hell," paddling specialist Brian Angwin quietly pointed out later. "All we did was drag our bloody asses up and down the hills for a day. The worst of it was running out of water. I stopped to take a leak and it came out brown because I was so dehydrated."

"That night," Davis says, picking up the story, "it was pissing rain and we were out of food. So we had to scab a bit off a Japanese team as we huddled in a shelter by the side of the road. Gaw, it was miserable."

The caves went by quickly. Then came a moment they had all been waiting for. After leaving the caves, the course featured one last mile of canoeing before the finish. Tired because it was the middle of the night and they had been going for almost twenty-four hours straight, the team got in the waiting (patched) boats and paddled wearily to the finish. As it came in sight, Angwin reached into his pack and removed a piece of extra weight he'd carefully packed inside. He had hauled it through the jungle, down rivers, and underground. It was the Australian flag.

As the two boats paddled into view of the TV cameras and flash-bulbs, Team Australia unfurled the colors and draped them between the two boats for all the world to see. It was a moment sublime and patriotic. "I stripped my pack down to nothing before this race," Angwin said later, nursing a cold beer. "Anything to shave a few ounces off what I had to carry through that God-awful jungle. But that flag . . . I'd carry that anywhere. I didn't mind that weight one bit. I know not all of Australia was watching us, but still, we were Team Australia and proud of it."

I flew home thinking of that finish, wondering just what it took to get there, moved immensely by the patriotism. Where Madagascar had been a sharply-etched personal experience, I felt like I had sleepwalked through Borneo, silently filled with an envy toward those brave enough to compete. If I ever ventured back to another Raid, I told myself, I would cross the line. It wasn't enough anymore to watch and hear second-hand the experiences of others. "The worst time was at night," Karen Fry of Team Australia had told me. "We'd be walking with our headlamps on, you know, and though we never saw or heard really big animals, when we'd shine our lights into the jungle we could always see eyes shining back at us."

Next time, I told myself, it would be very cool to be the one in the jungle at night, shining my headlight into the wild darkness, trying to quell the urge to bolt as I wonder what's looking back at me, sizing me up.

That's the addictive thing about seeing dreams come true: you begin to dream on a much bigger canvas. Leaving the corporate world was such a mental and emotional release that I felt supercharged in all areas of my life. It's true what they say about being your own boss, that you actually work harder than ever before. The difference is that I loved the work, so it didn't feel like work at all. I also spent more time with my family, and found that smiles and laughter came a lot easier. Dreams I'd buried for years, things like traveling around the world and writing a book and flying supersonically, suddenly they seemed possible. Not easy. Not immediate. But possible, given time and perseverance (a quality I was sorely lacking).

All my newfound dream of competing in the Raid needed was a catalyst to set it in motion. And it sparked in the most unlikely of places: Disneyland.

The park was closed to the public when photographer Tony DiZinno and I showed up at 7:30 on the morning of February 27 for press check-in. We were there to cover the Grand Opening of Indiana Jones and the Temple of the Forbidden Eye, a roller-coaster/jeep ride/cultural odyssey/dance-with-death through an exotic subterranean tomb, leaving every thirty seconds.

It was deathly silent as we made our way down Main Street. Disneyland and crowds are synonymous. Without them it feels smaller, intimate—not at all larger than life. There was a cool fog floating low to the ground, accenting the isolation. An employee began steam-cleaning the streets in front of Sleeping Beauty's castle, answering a long-held question of mine about how they keep the place looking so brand-new. "Even when the rides are off, the magic is still here," Tony said in a near whisper, soaking it all in.

It was true. Like a movie star still gorgeous without makeup, the park held us. We felt like intruders into a surprisingly magic kingdom. We sat down on a bench and said nothing, absorbing the still. It was one of those perfect moments you want to seize and put in your pocket for safekeeping, then trot out and relive when the world gets too crazy. Moments like that are few. They are also fleeting. After just five minutes of reverie crowds began filtering past, fellow journalists on their way to Indy. As if on cue, Tony and I stood up with a sigh. "Ready?" I asked, taking one last look around. The place was so perfect. Too bad they had to open it to the public.

"Ready," he agreed. And off we went into the crazed world of Indy. Built to look like a partially uncovered Angkor Wat, the temple loomed fifty feet away. But that was just the entrance, or the "preride" in Disney-speak. From there it would be a 300-yard descent into a narrow, low-ceilinged cavern before we actually boarded the ride. On a hot summer day I figured that would equate to roughly three hours of waiting, all the while sandwiched between cocoa-buttered, sweat-soaked tourists and their buzz-cut offspring. For the grand opening, however, it would mean just five minutes of brisk walking.

We passed through the entry portal, then wound through the narrow passageway that slowly brought us several stories underground. Emerging onto what looked like a replica of a subway platform, we were escorted onto a 1940s-era jeep with oversized tires, harnessed to an unseen track. The look and feel weren't mesmerizing from a thrill seeker's point of view, but had that passive ambiance Disney is noted for, effortlessly dropping our mindset into pre–World War II Morocco.

I love Disneyland, but that doesn't qualify me as a "ride guy." In other words, I don't whoop and holler and squeal like a stuck pig with every dip and undulation. Whooping and hollering is hard enough for me to accomplish in a thoroughly soundproofed bedroom. Going ballistic at the most public of amusement parks is out of the question.

But I did on Indy. There was the plunge into the temple, the swooping right and left turns that caused the jeep to roll almost to the point of tipping, the crossing of the rickety wooden bridge, the cobra that popped out of nowhere to attack the jeep, the explosions, the scurrying hordes of rats and spiders, and of course, the huge boulder, straight out of the first Indiana Jones movie, that rolled straight toward us before we took a radical, stomach-dropping detour. The part I liked best was when the ride passed through a long, dark tunnel, somehow triggering a hail of blow dart fire. OK, I knew the jets of air whistling past my head weren't really passing blow darts. And I know the "pings" against the jeep weren't errant shots, either. But it felt like it. And I ducked involuntarily. Every time. "You feel that?" Tony would yell above the very loud rumble of our jeeps. "I mean it, man. I could feel those darts going right past my head."

As we finally emerged, somehow unscathed, from the temple, I felt like I should have been wearing a Dramamine patch. My legs wobbled like I'd been at sea during a Force-12 gale. "I feel like I just spent time in a paint shaker," Tony mumbled, touching one hand to his forehead.

Then, because we were feeling very much like two journalistic professionals, and in that vein felt obligated to cover the story from soup to nuts, leaving no stone unturned in pursuit of excellence, we turned around and got back on that bucking monstrosity. And rode it again and again and again. When we finally emerged into the daylight for good, Disneyland was open to the public. And while the quaint wonder of a private Disneyland was no more, I found myself stuck on the thought that, while Indiana Jones was wonderful, experiencing the same perils would be all the more exciting if I were working without a net. In other words, if the danger were real, and if the safe passage back to the real world took days and nights of exhaustive physical labor, fording rivers, and climbing over mountains.

CHAPTER 4

Oklahoma and Other Delights

Everything changed after Borneo. The sport was clearly getting bigger. When Steines rented a theater on the Paramount Studios back lot to preview his documentary, the place was packed. "Adventure racing" had also split into two worlds. One was the Raid, which wandered wherever it pleased on the globe with the exception of North America. Burnett bought the North American rights to the Raid from Fusil in 1992. The agreement required Fusil to contribute operational and marketing expertise on a consulting basis. At the same time, Fusil was precluded from conducting events or soliciting sponsors in the United States. However, the driven and visionary personalities of Burnett and Fusil doomed their relationship from the start. They spoke very little in Borneo, then dissolved the relationship altogether—after Burnett made a furtive, rebuffed attempt to take over worldwide Raid operations. The two subsequently ended their relationship in court. Results are sealed.

THEN THERE was the Eco-Challenge, shiny and new, ready to fling itself into the American consciousness between April 25 and May 6, 1995. Burnett's cramped Topanga Canyon office was exchanged for a thirty-third-floor suite in tony Universal City Plaza. Burnett and Terkelsen sold television rights to MTV (whose parent company, Viacom, owned Universal City Plaza—thus the swell office space), guaranteeing that their race would even have a different look on video.

Instead of the long, slow pans and painful close-ups favored by Marenco, the French production company filming the Raid, Eco would be all "shaky-cam"—handheld, brief snippets, in your face while simultaneously distant in a very hip way. "The genie," Burnett took to saying, "is out of the bottle."

The question of political correctness also came into being for the first time when adventure racing was moved to the States. The course was in southwestern Utah, and environmentalists were afraid competitors would trounce sacred desert land. *Backpacker* magazine, in its April 1995 issue, devoted a scathing editorial to the question of whether adventure racers belonged in the great outdoors. The writer called the desert a church, a place where Eco-hooligans should not be allowed to tread. There was some imperiousness to the words: *Backpacker* plainly felt that its obviously more sensitive, aesthetic-minded readership should be allowed to hike through the desert and anywhere else they please.

Spurred on by the editorial, a group of extremists made anonymous phone calls, threatening to blow up the Eco course or shoot contestants. Something called the Southwest Utah Wilderness Alliance (SUWA) lobbied the Utah congressional delegation in Washington, D.C., to prevent Eco from taking place. Their efforts were countered by Utah state officials who saw Eco as a shot in the arm for tourism (ironically, the state officials were also promining and prodevelopment). It was a tense standoff, with much ado being made about single-file lines of competitors tramping on foot through land devastated daily by four-wheel-drive vehicles and cattle grazing.

In the end, both sides felt they'd won. The race was allowed to progress. But to be extra eco-friendly, Burnett was held to stiff environmental stipulations, including minimal use of helicopters and a requirement that teams defecate into plastic bags, then carry those bags to assistance points for proper disposal. The trotting out of the poo would become the competitors' main gag. Those suffering constipation would become suspects of low-grade eco-terrorism.

With that kind of mindset prevalent, it's small wonder Fusil preferred the lack of scrutiny of competing in less-developed countries. No one blinked an eye when his helicopters scared millions of bats from the Mulu Caves in the middle of the day, and yet the same inept happenstance in Utah would have been an *Outside* feature.

The problem was one of changing public approaches to the great outdoors. Old-school environmentalists have long had the backcountry all to themselves. They feel proprietary about overgrown deer trails in the middle of nowhere. They're the ones who have fought the battles over the years, however, going to court by sending their dollars to the Sierra Club and Audubon Society, making sure development takes a backseat to public use of pristine open land. This is how Teddy Roosevelt envisioned the national parks when he created them at the turn of the century. By virtue of the dogma, perseverance, and sacred attitude toward out-of-the-way wilderness (as opposed to Yosemite or Yellowstone wilderness, where concession stands and laundromats cater to weekend warriors), old-school environmentalists can rightfully claim a sense of ownership about public lands.

The problem is, they're still public. And Joe Six-Pack with an RV has just as much right to access as old-school, Edward Abbey–toting backpackers. But Joe can only go so far in his RV, because he needs the electrical hookups. In that way, there has always been peace in the backcountry between two very disparate groups of individuals. Joe Six-Pack stayed in the parking lot, never hiking more than a mile or two; old-school types parked (preferably on the opposite side of the parking lot from Joe Six-Pack), then hiked as quickly as possible into the solitude of the wilderness.

The advent of mountain biking in the 1970s and 1980s changed all that. First developed on Mount Tamalpais in Marin County, California, by reckless thrill seekers with too much time on their hands, mountain biking was a bastardization of two very pure forms. The first was the balloon-tired beach cruiser. With wide handlebars and heavy steel frame geometry, the beach cruiser was almost indestructible.

The second borrowed form was the racing bike. Often called the ten-speed, racing bikes are lightweight and too fragile for off-road use, with gearing systems designed to make hill climbing easier. By grafting ten-speed gears onto beach cruisers, pioneers like Gary Fisher and Otis Guy found their behemoths attained a functional ability beyond cruising the boardwalk on a sunny afternoon. Beach cruisers were suddenly perfect for climbing fire roads. Narrows trails, dubbed "singletrack," previously used only by trail runners and backpackers, became the scene of serious high-speed excitement as "mountain bikers" bounced their big balloon tires over ruts and divots and off jumps.

Soon the sport spread beyond Marin. Bikes were altered, made more lightweight. Races began. First, casually. Then, organized under the auspices of the National Off-Road Bicycling Association (NORBA). Champions like Ned Overend and John Tomac popularized the sport, which soon spread to Europe. By 1996, when it was first contested as an Olympic sport (and wholly dominated by the cycling-mad Euros), more mountain bikes were sold worldwide than any other type of bicycle. Though studies showed that only one in ten mountain bike owners ever ventured off the pavement, the idea of mountain bikes had become so popular and so connected with extreme outdoor adventure that companies like Mountain Dew and Taco Bell were featuring mountain bikers in advertisements.

Mountain biking's popularity affected both wilderness land use and old-school environmentalists in big ways. First, quiet outdoor spots few had ever heard of, like Durango and Moab and Mammoth, became mountain biking hotbeds. Not a summer day went by that a mountain biker wasn't running some old-school backpacker off a trail. Politely, in most cases, but for a group of men and women who'd cut their teeth on solitude in the backcountry, sharing a trail with anything other than grizzly bears and mule deer was maddening.

Second, mountain bikers came in numbers. They were sociable types, apt to snag five or twenty friends and cycle fifty miles into the middle of nowhere just for fun. Joe Six-Pack never did that.

And finally, mountain bikers were young. Their attitudes and music and clothes lacked the hippy funk and '60s ideals so prevalent among old-school sorts. Body piercing instead of bushy beards. PowerBars instead of granola. The times, they were a-changin'.

So old-schoolers could be excused when they put up a stink about Burnett and Terkelsen's idea to route 225 Eco-racers through Utah's red-rocked church. Endangered peregrine falcon aeries near the course, and bighorn sheep in the middle of lambing season only added fuel to the fire. Eco had the potential for full-scale environmental war between the old school and new school of outdoor land management. Both sides were passionate about their point of view. The threat of booby trappers and snipers was very real.

Eco would be held through the canyon lands of Utah and down the

Colorado River, finishing on Lake Powell. The number of competitors would be large in a most American way: seventy-five teams, almost double the Raid. The number of journalists would be similarly large. And because restrictions by the Bureau of Land Management limited the number of helicopters organizers could use, the press was to be guided around in a four-wheel-drive tour bus. The mere thought made me claustrophobic. Journalistically, I can think of no worse way of getting a story than being sheparded around by race management, steered toward what they want you to see, and far away from anything smacking of controversy. So I decided against requesting a credential. I would grab a few friends and road trip out to the course. There would be a security issue—due to the environmentalists' threats, Utah State Police were guarding the course. This only made for a more offbeat adventure in my mind.

"IT'S SO WIDE open out here, that sometimes an accident'll happen on the highway and we won't discover it for a few days. Had one last month—van overturned. Everybody was thrown out, musta been fifteen of them." The Utah sheriff cast an eye across the desert west of Moab. Midthirties, ungroomed blond mustache, probably a tackle or guard when he played high school football. The type of guy that enjoys a plate of bacon and eggs and a bottomless cup of coffee at the local diner before pointing his four-wheel-drive into the desert for a day of beauty and tragedy. But he wasn't a simple man, and he didn't talk easily about the death he witnessed. Some of it was murder, some accidental, some self-inflicted. But the common thread was the absolute isolation of the Utah desert. A land with a Biblical look, where witnesses were hard to come by.

Sometimes, he told me, once we got on the subject of grisly accidents, he'd spot perfectly good cars parked miles from nowhere. Seemingly abandoned. But he'd know—and he pointed this out in that confidential, matter-of-fact way that cops used to talk about death—that when he drove over to investigate it would be something else. Suicide, most likely, and without a note. A frustrated someone afraid to do it where their loved ones might find the body.

The sheriff rambled on about the phenomenon of the desert, of how the red-rocked nothingness provoked awe among those seeking it, and abject despair in others. The conversation spun around on itself until we were talking about that freeway wreck again. "Yes, sir," he chuckled softly, gazing again toward Moab in a way that told me he was one of those who saw majesty in the red rocks. "There was bodies scattered from hell to breakfast."

"Southeastern Utah's so wide open that it swallows you whole," he was saying, though I didn't know until I got there. I came with three others, closer to strangers than friends, brought together by common curiosity. We left Southern California on a Wednesday night, hoping to intercept the athletes near Green River, where the race crossed under Highway 70. Our drive east was in a full-sized van stocked with Red Vines, Gatorade, topographic maps, and the best loud music money could buy. Keri Puhl, a level-headed, enigmatic promotions coordinator for the Tinley apparel company was our driver. Sean Scott, a wry, earringed sort, flopped on a beanbag in the seatless cargo area. I did the same. Don Baker, a former Navy SEAL and San Diego SWAT officer, rode shotgun. I would soon find that it was a group comfortable with both searching and sophomoric conversation, and with rambling adventure.

Our mission was twofold. First, to see how Eco compared with the Raid, which in turn would be a forecast of the future of adventure racing in America. Second, whether or not claims made by local environmental groups about the adventure athletes doing irrevocable damage to the desert had any foundation. There was a chance we might not even see the race. We discussed that between snatches of sleep and choruses of Johnny Cash's "Delia" as we drove Interstate 15 through the night. We were glib in referring to our trip as a "guerrilla" excursion, but the fact was that we might not be entirely welcome. Both the State of Utah and event organizers were promising heavy security to prevent outside groups from doing damage. That meant road blocks and ID checks, especially at areas where contestants would congregate. In effect, we had no identification to prove we belonged any more than a potential booby-trapper. Whether or not we would be able to breach the ring of security (which came to mean sheriffs, park rangers, and Burnett's own hired muscle) was a legitimate concern.

"You here for the race?" the waitress at the Red Rock Cafe in

Hanksville asked. It was our last stop before detouring to the race site. She set down coffee before the men, hot chocolate in front of Keri.

"Yeah," we replied in unison, lowering our eyes. The guerrilla thing was making us a bit paranoid. We were doing everything but affecting accents and pasting on fake beards.

"What, uh, what's the local attitude?" I ventured. She didn't look like the type that would call the cops. "Are they on the side of the racers or the environmental groups?"

"Personally, I'm an environmentalist." She put her order pad away. Old enough to have enjoyed the sixties, but too young for retirement, the waitress had a bit too much urbanite in her manner for remote Hanksville. I guessed she'd probably moved there from Vegas or Salt Lake City, trading hustle-bustle for regular doses of pure silence. She continued: "But the whole thing reminds me of the movie *Oklahoma*. Remember that one?"

Not really, but I'd seen a very clever spoof on *Sesame Street* in which Kermit demonstrated the vowels by alternately singing "A-kla-homa," "E-klahoma," and so on. I chose not to share that memory. "Remember that the sheep men and cattle men didn't exactly see eye to eye, but they had to learn to get along because it was better for everybody? Well, that's how I see this race."

Variations on this theme would be echoed by everyone from park rangers to deputies in the days to come. Conservative elements in the Utah legislature were eyeing the protected land around Hanksville as a source of potential mining and development revenue. Locals, who didn't cotton to the idea that any of it would bring about new jobs, were hoping that the exposure Eco-Challenge would bring would cause a public outcry that would, in turn, force Congress to preserve it forever.

The spot we'd chosen to make our entrance was roughly the halfway point of the course. Before reaching us, competitors would ride horseback for a day, navigate water-filled canyons by moonlight, then trek for 110 miles. After passing through our location at race headquarters, they would alternately mountain bike, rappel, climb, whitewater raft, and canoe to the finish in Lake Powell.

Leaving Hanksville (never again to be referred to as "Hicksville" after the waitress's eloquence), we drove the final twenty miles to the race, detouring from Highway 24 onto a dirt road. Five miles farther down, a sea of fluorescent tents and four-wheel-drive vehicles near the base of a square-topped butte marked the spot. Like sentinels, a line of electric-blue porta-potties stood watch on a rise, their color standing out in sharp contrast to the deep crimson butte.

A swarthy, goateed New Yorker guarding the entrance held up a hand as we approached. Keri was driving. I felt nervous for some reason, which was ridiculous. We were on public lands, in the middle of majesty, with no conceivable consequence for our impudence beyond being told to turn around (whence we would simply find a less confrontational method of observing the event). Still, I was nervous, and could feel the electric silence that told me the others were too.

Keri pulled to a stop. She rolled down her window. The New Yorker stuck his head in. He swiveled it left and right as if searching for contraband. "Can I help you?"

"Hi," Keri purred. "We're here for the race." She smiled at the guy. He smiled back.

"Who are you?" He was flirting now, looking only at Keri. A silent spell had been cast over Don and me. I dared not speak or even breathe too loudly for fear something might destroy this wonderful performance of Keri's.

Sean had no such fears: "We're journalists, dammit. All four of us, we're journalists and we're here to cover the race. We want to tell the whole story." Keri tried not to look ruffled, and she kept that smile of hers pasted in place. But her eyes narrowed just enough for me to know that she wanted to bust Sean in the chops. This was her moment to shine, after all, not his to ruin.

The guy looked hard at her. "Journalists?" He said it the way someone else might have said "serial killers." There was no reason for it, but I'm sure that someone, at some time, warned him that the media is a monster that has to be contained. I didn't take it personally.

Keri recovered quickly enough to point out that I was the only journalist (withering glare from Mister Broadway here), but that the other three . . . why, they were hard-working members of the apparel industry. Sean, well, wasn't he quite the practical joker?

"All right then. Have a good time." And so the Eco-adventure progressed in earnest.

For some reason, I thought we would do something special when we got to headquarters. Maybe ingrain ourselves into a hub of activity, or even find something exotic to observe. But though there were people performing all types of organizational activity, the only thing really to do was observe the race, which was as exciting as watching paint dry because the teams were halfway through that 110-mile walk. Maybe if they were on some scenic trail overlooking the nearby Colorado River it might have been more inspiring. But Bureau of Land Management restrictions prohibited off-road travel by contestants. Grazing by cattle was allowed, and they were everywhere the contestants weren't, chewing the sparse grass and looking largely unaffected by the raw wind that raked over from the Rockies. But competitors were confined to dirt roads. It smacked of compromise—the Bureau, environmentalists, and race organizers finding a way to make the race happen. And while I knew that holding a major adventure race in America made compromise necessary, there was something about sending teams down dirt roads. The competitors were every bit as tough as at the Raid, if a bit more intense in a gung-ho sort of way. This showed that the concept translated. But after all that time and effort to get to the Eco-Challenge—securing Bureau of Land Management maps, lining up the van, taking time away from my family—I was bored by the end of the first day.

Yet my mood changed after a good night's sleep. I awoke the next morning well before dawn. Surrounded by a land without complication, I felt awash in a sort of spiritual awareness. Life was so simple, it seemed. There was no wind, no sound. I put my clothes on and took a walk. First, into a deep ravine, then upward, all the way to the top of a mesa. I couldn't explain the overwhelming connection I felt with all that surrounded me, but I found myself striving to keep my thoughts pure and uncomplex. The sensation that all I was going through was somehow connected—the Raid, the road trip, the morning walk—was pervasive, and I wanted to seize it for all it was worth. Such total peace visits only occasionally.

I walked back down to the ravine, to where I knew water flowed, and bathed in the pale morning light. The sky was flat and low, tinged reddish gray. I stood naked in the ravine, pouring freezing water over my head and hands and heart, and wishing that my traveling buddies would sleep late, so that I might know the wonderful silence and sense of connection longer.

It's easy when writing about an event to spend so much time analyzing that you lose sight of the reason people compete in the first place. That's what happened to me initially in Utah. Maybe because there wasn't a twenty-hour plane flight or passport control to mark passage, I found myself scrutinizing the race organization and searching for comparisons to the Raid more than noting competitors. I saw the MTV people from New York looking so out of place, so urban with their busy body language. And I saw Mark Burnett flying about in his helicopter, keeping the race from descending into chaos. There were hordes of journalists, tons of assistance teams, rows of porta-potties (the electric blue sentinels were obviously eyesores, but just as obviously necessary to avert a small-scale environmental catastrophe), and even a pizza place down the road in Green River. So, no, the Eco-Challenge wasn't the Raid Gauloises. But it was never intended to be. Eco was deliberately American in flavor, imbued with the frantic energy of people new at something, solving a set of problems for the first time. Eco was different, but equal. Here to stay.

Beyond that, Utah. No matter how glossy or glitzy or MTV Eco could feel at times, the fact remained that competitors were marching through some of the most demanding terrain anywhere. Water was scarce, wind fierce, isolation on the desert total. The despair the Utah deputy pointed out was evident in competitors. Not so much the French teams like Hewlett-Packard and Lestra Sport, nor veterans like Cathy Sassin-Smith. They possessed the experience and reserves to avert their gaze from the endless horizon as they trekked. No, the teams that suffered were mostly those who'd seen Steines' ESPN show or *Dateline* and thought adventure racing was simply a very long triathlon. Most of them quit. Those who continued to the final seventy-mile canoe leg down the Colorado River into Lake Powell all echoed the same postrace comment: this is the toughest thing I've ever done in my life. And if considered from no other perspective than this overwhelming mass empowerment, Eco was a rousing competitive success.

The environmental impact was assessed by writer Daniel Glick in the July/August issue of *Eco-Traveler* magazine: "When the race ended, though, I had to wonder if there weren't more pressing issues for these environmental groups to spend their resources on. Given the number of threats to the wild nature of the Colorado Plateau from more boom-and-bust development proposals, why didn't they tap into the energy and publicity from the event to make people aware of the real, long-term effects to the region: from multinational companies seeking to mine coal on the Kaiparowits plateau; to oil and gas exploration that would suck every last drop of energy from the grounds, no matter the cost to the ecosystem; and real estate developers who build subdivisions with lawns first and worry about finding water later? The real threat to Utah isn't events like the Eco-Challenge, but the prevalent Manifest Destiny attitude that would provide unfettered access to this magical region to everybody, everywhere, for every purpose, at all times."

Later, when the MTV documentary aired and the magazines stories came out, Eco's future was secured. People no longer talked about the race where people had the bad feet, they gave it a name: adventure racing. And just one adventure race came to mind, the Eco-Challenge. Within three months Burnett had already filled the seventy-five-team roster for the second Eco, in British Columbia a year later.

Hard on the heels of Utah, other adventure-races sprouted in America. ESPN threw adventure racing into their brand new Extreme Games. Burnett coordinated the course. Contestants adventure-raced the dense, blackfly-infested woods of Maine. Don Baker, my road trip buddy, who'd been tossing around the idea of putting on his own race for some time, teamed up with Adidas in mid-June. The Triple Bypass represented a new type of adventure race, the one-day event. Events were bike, run, paddle, and a pair of mystery events (log carry, target shooting) bearing great similarity to his SEAL days. The race drew fifty teams.

Within one year, adventure racing had gone from a sport without a name to the fastest growing outdoor sport in America. The public, the press, and anyone with anything to do with outdoor apparel adored it.

A week after Eco ended, Fusil held a press conference in San Diego to announce the Argentine region of Patagonia as the site of the 1995 Raid. It was, he said, the perfect spot. Stung by Samling's record finish in Borneo, Fusil guaranteed that Patagonia would last at least eight days, maybe more. The events would be ice-climbing, horseback riding, cross-country skiing, kayaking, and whitewater canoeing.

I had had dinner with Fusil in March. Still a working journalist, he was in San Diego to cover the America's Cup for French radio, and had flown in directly from Raid reconnaissance in Patagonia. We ate at a seaside fish restaurant. Over Merlot and scallops, he let slip a secret of the Raid: "The special thing is not the winning, but the adventure. I love the adventure. When I sailed the Atlantic [aboard a four-man catamaran, Fusil set a record for fastest Atlantic sail crossing of nine days in 1991] it was not for the record, although that was very important. It was for the adventure. The most exciting thing was not the calm but the storms. You see, when you go for a record, you must wait until there is a storm in New York. You leave during the storm and it stays with you all the way across the Atlantic. But there is a point well off the coast of England where the storms always disappear. If you do not get another storm coming up from Africa, you cannot get the record. So you pray for the storm."

Pray for the storms.

He also spoke glowingly of Patagonia, of clear rivers and brown trout as big as your arm and untouched beauty. It is as remote and unchanged as the American West of the late nineteenth century. Cowboys—gauchos, in this case—still ride the range, tending to cattle and sheep. Instead of the Rockies, the Andes mountains rise precipitously from the flat nothingness of the arid brown midwest plains. The sides of the mountains are ringed with pine forests, the tops haloed in snow and ice and giant chips of gray rock. The rivers run aquamarine, as if someone had dyed them to a perfect hue. The wind, a factor synonymous with Patagonia, blows so hard across the top of the Andes that Argentine pilots have sworn it pushed their jet fighters backward. When I would finally arrive in Patagonia in November, the most common thought I had was that if it weren't so remote—if Patagonia were nestled somewhere near, say, the Napa Valley—tour buses would overrun and decimate it, just like they do every place else where natural beauty equates to tourism. But Patagonia is so close to the bottom of the world and so far off the beaten path that its beauty is virginal. There are few roads through the Andes, and most of those close for the winter. Patagonia is a throwback to a time when natural beauty wasn't quantified by dollar signs.

"Patagonia," he added ominously, "will be the hardest Raid ever. I guarantee that."

But how hard? Everyone was finishing adventure races. In 1989, the handful finishing the first Raid were considered the hardiest of souls. Since then, the percentage of teams finishing the Raid and Eco had crept up to ten, then twenty, then almost fifty percent. Toughest race in the world? Debatable anymore. Pretty soon everyone would be finishing, just like with marathons and the Hawaii Ironman. Maybe Raid and Eco courses were getting easier, not so bent toward studliness, ensuring better PR and warm feelings all around.

Which ultimately begged the question, had the Raid Gauloises ever been the toughest race on earth? Or was that mere hype, the sort fabricated by would-be adventurers like me who idealized the competition simply because it was unusually grueling?

With the dream in motion, it was time to find out by making it come true. Looking back, what amazes me most is that I somehow thought the process would be easy. More incredibly, I thought it would be painless.

PART II

How Not To Do an Adventure Race

CHAPTER 5

What It Feels Like
To Quit the Raid

As they carried me to the medevac helicopter that freezing Argentine morning, a wholly unwanted image flooded my mind. I thought of Madagascar, where I had watched a normally stoic German team break down after circumstance forced them from the race. What puzzled me most as I watched the Germans was how a simple contest could force men of infinite masculinity to weep as if they had lost a loved one.

I ALSO remembered it was in Madagascar where I had seen a French squad abandon a teammate atop a towering windswept butte, at the same time abandoning their chances of winning. "She is a bitch," they shrugged in explanation, forgetting that they had trained together for almost a year, pledging allegiance for the Raid's arduous days and nights. At the time, I empathized with that lone woman. How must she have felt, I wondered, watching her teammates go on without her after all that physical and mental preparation?

In Patagonia, I found out. As the blue-and-white medevac helicopter lifted me from the course, I looked down from on high and saw my team continuing without me. The tears began to fall right about then. The Raid Gauloises, I realized, is much more than a simple race. How does it feel to quit the Raid Gauloises? Like a death.

CHAPTER 6

Let the Games Begin

Turning points always seem so clear, so sharp, in retrospect. But when they're actually occurring, their significance can be blurred by the vagaries of daily life, and their meaning lost until much later, when the mind's eye has had a chance to focus.

IT IS only now that I can make sense of one hot day in Sacramento, over twenty years ago. The course was flat, an out-and-back ten-miler on a riverfront bike trail. I was fourteen. My dad ran next to me, his flawless sense of pace keeping us unerringly at six-minute miles. Counting my position at the turnaround, I quietly noted I was third in my age group.

We weren't talking. Not necessarily because of the pace, but because my Dad and I never seemed to get around to talking, whether we were racing or not.

About my dad: Friends who have heard thumbnail sketches of us would jump to draw comparisons with Pat Conroy's fictional character, Bull Meechum, better known as the Great Santini.

There is a similarity—both my dad and Santini were career officers. Accomplished jet pilots. Devoted to their work. But my dad was never condescending to me the way Santini was toward his eldest son.

My dad began running in his mid-thirties to lose weight, but soon began winning his age group at local races. For me, running was similarly accidental; I scored well on the six-minute run in a sixth-grade gym class and never looked back. In junior high, I improved, winning in track and cross-country. But I was never as good as my dad.

I would watch him pull away from me whenever we raced the Sacramento road circuit. His speed was formidable, his metronome pace maddeningly smooth.

But the hallmark of my dad's running was his silence. When we ran workouts together—just the two of us, side by side for an hour or more—he wouldn't utter a word. Sometimes I suspected that he really didn't like me, and I was surprised when my mother once confided that my father treasured our runs. "He's just quiet," she insisted. "He loves to run with you." I understand now, because I've inherited that same contentment with silence. But I didn't then.

Then something happened that hot day along the Sacramento River. I had gotten better the past year while my dad was in Vietnam. As the miles passed, I could feel my strength building. Somewhere between miles six and seven I realized I could pick up the pace. Panic, bordering on terror, filled me. I knew I could catch those guys in front of me, but not if I continued to run with my dad.

A half-mile passed before I said anything. Butterflies the size of baseballs churned in my stomach. Never in my life had I passed him. Never. He was the best in our house at everything—running, Monopoly, chess . . . everything. Instead of happiness, I felt like I was taking an unwanted step toward manhood.

"Dad . . . ," I said finally. My throat was tight; the words strained. "I gotta go."

He was silent a moment. Then, in a voice unmistakably laced with pride, he calmly urged: "Go after'm, Marty."

And I was gone.

We didn't race together again for almost sixteen years. During those years, I slowly pushed away from my dad. It was a tumultuous time of rebellion and separation that dragged on much longer than it should have. Until I was twenty-nine, I generally avoided him. When we did see each other, little was said.

Then, at the Los Angeles Marathon in 1991, as I struggled by the eighteen-mile mark, my fast early pace fallen victim to heat and dehydration, my dad stepped quietly from the crowd. He was dressed to run. He'd planned to be there all along; had driven sixty miles to wait for me—to run with me.

"How do you feel?" he asked. It sounded like one man talking to another.

"Awful."

He laughed. "You can do it." God, I was glad to see him.

We ran together, my dad and I. And we began to talk.

The decision to become a Raid competitor was a turning point like that. It marked a sea change for me in ways I could not have foreseen. My life, and the way I viewed the world, would forever be altered, and in a most powerful and positive way.

The journey to Patagonia began in earnest in July 1995. A small group of us banded together as a Raid team. Susan Hemond and I were first. Susan was out of retirement after surgery corrected the source of her health problems, and she was eager to reestablish herself as the premier female adventure racer in America. Then there were Don Baker and an ex-Navy SEAL buddy of Don's named Mike Sammis, who would act as team navigator, and me. For the final member we hoped to lure a top climber, someone to lead us through Patagonia's peaks. Mike, an experienced rock climber himself, was close friends with some of the world's leading alpine experts. It was our hope that he could talk one into coming aboard. Fittingly, Jimmy Garfield, the alternate member of the first Team American Pride, would serve as alternate member of our team as well.

I was the moving force behind putting it all together and thus, somewhat uncomfortably (for Raid rules mandate such a position), selected myself team captain. It was my job to raise the money, select the team, acquire equipment, and get us to Patagonia.

We had our first team workout in July, a day-long trek up the backside of Saddleback in 100-degree heat, then another day kayaking the calm waters of Newport Bay. Team chemistry seemed perfect, with the mood light and conversation easy. No one had any physical problems. All in all, an auspicious start. Feeling slightly giddy, we even began to talk of not just finishing the Raid, but winning. Someone forgot to remind us of what happens when American teams make such predictions.

Meanwhile, I got the assignment of a lifetime: the chance to circumnavigate the globe aboard the Concorde. I liked the irony, the chance to fly around the world on the most modern transportation in contrast to the primitive throwbacks the Raid would soon offer. The team agreed that while I was doing the supersonic gig, they would travel to the Outdoor Retailer trade show in Reno. There, amid the backpacks and tents and hiking boots being promoted, they hoped to find a climber.

So . . . the Concorde. The whole world. In just over one day.

Ah, freelancing. It's a world that revolves around generating new story ideas. Sometimes they appear in the mind half-baked, needing a few hours of thought to round into something an editor might buy. But sometimes lightning strikes and they pop out of nowhere. A case in point: the fifteen-second Coors commercial in June that proclaimed a national contest to select passengers for an attempt at the around-the-world speed record. With any luck, the Air France Concorde would fly from New York to New York in slightly more than a day. I was so excited that I was on the phone to the marketing people at the Coors Brewery in Golden, Colorado, the next morning. Did they, I wanted to know, have room on board for journalists?

Of course. Journalists write stories and stories equate to publicity and publicity makes money. And everybody loves money. I hung up and called David. He and his wife had moved from Tokyo to Vancouver, so there was a very real possibility he could be a part of the Concorde experience. A phone call to Golden later, he was. Which is how the two of us came to be in New York on August 14, 1995, crammed into a ball-room of the JFK Hilton with eighty other passengers as part of a pre-flight pep rally. Donald Pevsner, the flight's coordinator, a towering man with a vainglorious streak as wide as the Concorde's delta wingspan, was desperately trying to impress upon us all the importance of our mission.

"This," Pevsner boomed from a midroom podium, "will be the greatest feat in aviation history since Lindbergh crossed the Atlantic!" Pevsner is a very nice man, but I knew he was destined for parody at some point in the trip. Comments like that weren't helping matters any.

David and I stood in back, munching hors d'oeuvres and quietly catching up while Pevsner rambled on about the exquisite nature of Concorde travel ("It discriminates against two types of people, the tall and the poor"). David surprised me by letting slip that he and Kaori were working on having a child. "No kidding," I said. David had always been loathe to give up his independence by having children. "Any plans for a name?"

"Nah. Not yet."

"Is she going to go back to work or stay home?"

"We haven't really talked about it yet."

"Will she be breast-feeding?" An odd question, unless you have children. Talking about another man's wife's bosom is de rigueur for fathers. Compared with the explicit nature of some birth videos I've seen, breast functions are a rather mild boundary to cross.

"I'm not sure," David replied, "I've been trying for five years. Nothing seems to come out."

Always good to see David. Standing in that ballroom, I was reminded of a curious fact: David is what I would consider a great friend. We swap stories about our wives, commiserate about the travails of freelance writing, share the joy of writing (there is a wondrous elation when a sentence or a paragraph or a story sings; all the bloodletting that makes it possible is suddenly worth it), and alert each other the moment a potential free trip comes along.

The funny thing is, we live a thousand miles from each other. The only time David and I hang out is while traveling. A more traditional definition of friendship is a neighbor or drinking buddy. David is neither. We meet in places like New York or Genoa or Tokyo, see a bit of the world, try to make each other laugh more often than we get on each other's nerves, then fly home, only to meet up again months or even a year later. It is a friendship founded on jet travel, impossible at any other time in history. An adventure on the Concorde, the ultimate in air travel, was somehow fitting.

"Listen up," Pevsner bellowed. David and I stopped our whispering. The first individuals to fly around the world, Pevsner wanted to tell us, were a cadre of Army Air Corps pilots back in 1924. It took them a whopping five months. Leaving from New York, our Concorde would arrive back just thirty-two hours and forty minutes later, traveling 25,351 statute miles and, it was hoped, squeaking past the current record of 32:48 set by another Concorde in 1992. En route there would be refueling and deplaning stops in Toulouse, Dubai, Bangkok, Guam, Honolulu, and Acapulco. Our cruising elevation would be a stratospheric 60,000 feet, so high that the earth's curvature would be visible below, and the heavens black instead of blue above. Our average speed would be nearly twice the speed of sound, or roughly 1,100 miles per hour—faster than a speeding bullet. "We'll see three sunrises and three sunsets," he exulted, "something only astronauts usually witness."

Despite Pevsner's enthusiasm, I had mixed feelings. As the son of a career pilot, I was weaned on aviation history. So on the one hand I was cognizant that what we were attempting—to be blunt: flying around the world in a souped-up bus—barely qualifies as a junket, let alone an achievement superior to the Battle of Britain, breaking the sound barrier, Arc Light, and man on the moon. Not to mention that it minimizes the death of Amelia Earhart, who disappeared following the same eastward route.

On the other hand, flying around the world supersonically is an E-ticket nonpareil. And though the idea of being a world record holder under less than epic conditions felt grossly illegitimate, Pevsner's twisted logic about our importance made vague sense. No, this wasn't on the scale of Lindbergh, but it was very cool nonetheless.

Even in this era, when manned spaceflight is ho-hum, the roster of Mach 2 fliers is limited to military personnel, astronauts (who orbit the earth at a speed closer to Mach 17), and Concorde passengers. The group is vaguely elitist, supersonic flight implying as it does either big money or big cojones.

My passion as a child was jet airplanes. I was inclined to do whatever it took to see aircraft up close. At one Air Force base where we lived my brother Matt and I even crawled through several hundred yards of tall grass (to avoid getting nabbed by base police) to stand at runway's end as an F-4 Phantom took off. We were so close that just before the pilot pushed the throttles forward he looked over at us. I still see his helmeted face, patently confused as to what a ten-year-old and eleven-year-old could possibly be doing just twenty yards from his plane.

I always wanted to be a jet pilot myself, but I never got around to actually entering the military (a niggling prerequisite). Yet I have never lost the hankering to go supersonic. One story I've been chasing for years is the chance to fly in the backseat of an F-14. Maybe some day it'll happen. In the meantime, there was the Concorde. And while we would never get inverted, nor flirt with death at treetop level in such an ungainly jet (incredible speeds aside, the Concorde is still a passenger aircraft, not a fighter), the fact remained: we were flying around the world. That such a thing is possible boggles the mind. It took Columbus three months to sail from Europe to the West

Indies. We would cover that distance in less time than it took him to weigh anchor.

I decided to wait until the flight was over to determine whether or not a record of this sort actually felt like a real world record, or just another one of those gimmicks on par with the man who stuffed a gross of live ferrets in his pants then phoned the people at Guinness.

"It's a world of hope. . . . "

I don't know how far it is from Saddleback Mountain to Toulouse. But I know for sure that aboard the Concorde Toulouse is exactly three hours and two beverage services from New York, where the thrust of takeoff pushed me far deeper into my seat than any 747 ever will. As we deplaned in that rural French city, my thoughts were as far away from blisters and deprivation as they have ever been. Instead, I was thinking record. World record. With just eight minutes separating the current mark and our estimated circumnavigation, our only hope of beating it revolved around split-second timing. "Listen up, people," Pevsner scolded over the intercom before we deplaned. We were cattle to the man and we didn't mind in the least. "I need you back in this aircraft not more than forty minutes from now."

He need not have worried. The mood in the cabin was one of out-right enthusiasm. We were eager and driven, sure that the Concorde—our Concorde—would catapult us into the Guinness book. And none of us would jeopardize that. Nobody would tarry in duty-free. No one would brawl with a Customs official or get lost somewhere in the air-port. There wasn't a soul among us who wanted to be the idiot delaying the trip in any way.

So we rushed in and out of Toulouse, where the first-ever Concorde flight took place on March 2, 1969. Thousands lined the runway in the darkness of a warm summer night, their flashbulbs popping as we landed. Then repressive Dubai, where we couldn't deplane until the Coors Light logo on the outside of the plane was covered with white tape; then Bangkok, where native girls presented us with sweetly scented flower bracelets and performed a ceremonial dance that involved balancing on one leg. We became a sovereign orbiting nation unto ourselves. In-flight we passed the time eating and drinking, strolling the aisles, snatching catnaps, watching the comings and goings of the sun, making new friends, and reading. I reveled in Peter Mayle's *A Year in Provence*. Celebrity passenger Tom Stafford, the astronaut who orbited the world in less than an hour aboard Apollo 10, read *Lost Moon*, the story of Apollo 13. Kyle Petty, the stock car driver, read Kafka.

"It's a world of cheer. . . . "

Cheer, indeed. Generally speaking, "world record attempt" conjures images of deprivation and discipline.

There's a different "D" word aboard the Concorde: Decadent, and remarkably so. Every meal—and there were seven, featuring everything from lobster to Sevruga caviar to tournedos—was cooked to French-chef perfection. The flight attendants wore Nina Ricci–designed uniforms, accompanied by the sort of subtle perfume that even uneducated noses pinpoint as expensive. All seats were first class. The wine list was full of velvety textures and fruity bouquets. Champagne, vodka, and cold Coors Light flowed like a river. My glass was not once dry. The Concorde flight crew, bless them, seemed to have a sixth sense about helping passengers develop and indefinitely maintain the perfect buzz. Though I teetered close to the edge, I never stepped over the edge into inebriation.

"Tell me," I discreetly inquired of a flight attendant, trying to discern if every sort of sensual pleasure had been experienced aboard the Concorde. I was reclining in her jumpseat amidships, drinking beer with David and trying to divine which magazines might be interested in Raid stories for 1995. We were dividing the magazine world between us, a process we called "Yalta." "Have you ever seen . . . uh, you know . . . two . . . go into the restroom together?"

She answered in an elegant English, but the reply was typically French in its matter-of-factness. "Twice. It was the same couple," and here she paused for emphasis, "before and after dinner. The second time they came out, the woman even winked at me."

Our new French confidante leaned closer. "I do not know how they did it. I have tried to imagine it many times, but I think there is no room." Whence she walked away, leaving us to peer into the microscopic lavatory, fantasizing about the precarious dynamics and gravitational forces necessary for Concorde sex.

For all that, however, the Concorde's true sensuality lies in the visceral sensation of flat-out speed. It is felt most keenly soon after the electric-blue Mach-meter lodged in the forward bulkhead reads "0.88." The afterburners kick in then, and with such force that it feels as if the hand of God is giving the aircraft an Almighty shove. The Mach-meter climbs quickly from there: 0.91, 0.95, 0.99. It hovers, teasing. Suddenly, 1.01. And somewhere far below, a sonic boom punctuates the moment our fully catered missile leaps to the far side of the sound barrier.

The clouds slip past in a blur over there.

"There's so much that we share. . . . "

The second half of the world was toughest. We were spent. A slave to circadian rhythms, I found myself catnapping involuntarily, awakening to my head drooped over my chest and a suave string of drool spilling out of the left side of my mouth. When the sun rose, like it did just before landing in Bangkok, I was as wide awake as if I'd gotten twelve hours of sleep. When it set just three hours later as we landed in Guam, I was nodding off, exhausted.

The sun and Donald Pevsner were our task masters, but we were a mutinous bunch by the time we landed in Guam. Enthusiasm was replaced by grouchy yearnings to get the damned thing over with. And though we appreciated the incredible effort of the personnel at Andersen Air Force Base, who greeted Petty like one of their own ("Hi, Kyle, come on over here. I'd like you to meet my General") and refueled us with the speed and professionalism of a NASCAR pit crew, it meant that we were off the ground in less than an hour. Our time outside the plane was a mere fifteen minutes. Good for the record, bad for the passengers. Stale air and claustrophobia were making our sleek tube feel like a sealed mine shaft.

It got worse in Honolulu, where Customs officials wouldn't allow us to deplane at all. Instead we sat in our seats on the humid tarmac, sweating, without drink service. Refueling took longest there, of course, over an hour and a half, both jeopardizing the record and heightening the claustrophobia. It was the low point, and we couldn't escape the island paradise fast enough. A group of marketing executives (mysteriously known as the "fuckin'-A boys") two rows behind me began a fart war as entertainment. I fled as soon as take-off allowed us to move around freely, but the war had touched us all by then. The mood in the cabin was downright hostile.

A new crew of flight attendants (the two cockpit crews—one flying, one sleeping in a cordoned section at the aircraft's rear—would remain on board the entire flight) came on board in Honolulu. Their rested faces and freshly creased uniforms were in every way a contrast with us bleary, rumpled passengers.

"Once we get a little closer to Acapulco," one passenger from Baton Rouge mumbled in a Cajun baritone. Refugees, we had fled to the very back of the plane. "I'm gonna drink me some whiskey. Things are gettin' a little crazy inside this thang."

"It's a. . . . "

The singing began two hours after we left the mariachis and margaritas of Acapulco, on final approach into JFK, when Pevsner—our Pevsner—confirmed over the loudspeaker what we'd all been wondering. "Ladies and Gentlemen, by my calculations we will break the record by over an hour," he announced proudly. There was applause. Cheering. Hugs and handshakes. The fuckin'-A boys pulled a bottle of hooch out of somewhere and passed it around.

From my seat in the second row I heard the melody coming from the rear cabin. It was that annoying song you can never, ever get out of your head, but now it was sweetly appropriate. Quickly, it worked its way to the front, until the whole supersonic party bus was grinning and singing. We had done it, all of us, in just under thirty-one hours and thirty minutes. Happy chills of camaraderie ran down my spine as I joined in: "It's a small world after all; it's a small world after all; it's a small world after all; it's a small, small world. . . ."

"How's it feel it be a world record holder?" said another passenger, shaking my hand.

"Awesome," I replied, taking one last gulp of champagne. "Let's take another lap."

Life was good. We were hustled off the plane, then through Customs. Probably because I was sitting in the second row, close to the door of the plane, and probably because I instinctively rush to clear Customs, I was the first passenger to gain official readmission to the United States.

Immediately, an airport official grabbed me by the arm and

gestured for me to follow. He was gruff in a New York way and I was sure I was in trouble of some sort. Maybe he knew about the flowered bracelet from Thailand I'd almost smuggled in. He walked quickly—very quickly—down a corridor, with me struggling to keep up. "C'mon, c'mon," he would say, looking back over his shoulder to make sure he hadn't lost me. After 100 yards we took a sharp left. He flung open a door, stepped inside, and yelled to someone I could not see: "Here he is!"

I gulped. They really did know about that damned bracelet. Visions of body cavity search, and not enough money to make bail.

But my worries were dispelled when I looked through the open door. The New York media waited impatiently on the other side. There were at least fifteen reporters and photographers, complete with a bank of microphones, video cameras, and very bright lights. "Step up to the microphones, please," one of them called in a bored voice.

So it was that I held my first press conference. How was the flight? What did we eat? How high did we fly? Was it fun? Would I do it again? David emerged from Customs a few minutes later and took a picture of the ironic scene of journalist getting interviewed by journalist. I have it framed now, hanging on a wall in my office.

While it had taken just thirty-one hours to fly all the way around the world on the fastest form of modern transportation, it would take at least eight days to travel just 300 miles in Patagonia, using modes of transport centuries old. So what had started off as a fantastic magazine assignment and decadent respite from the demands of Raid training, was in fact a startling counterpoint— Yin to the Raid's Yang—to what I hoped to achieve in Patagonia. It was a small world after all, I realized, but soon it would seem impossibly big.

I got back to the JFK Hilton, exhausted from over a day of being awake. The adrenaline buzz from the trip was so great that I couldn't sleep. I tossed and turned for an hour, then finally flipped on ESPN and called my office to check messages. There was one from Sue: The team had found a climber.

AS SUMMER moved into fall, I would find that a team is a constantly evolving relationship, no different from any other. That includes the requirement for transition. The addition of our climber stood as one of the biggest. It marked our leap from wanna-be pretenders to legitimate contenders.

It isn't possible to overestimate how much importance I placed on having a solid lead climber. Patagonia was projected to be one mountaineering feat after another, with climbing on rock and ice and glaciers as a standard part of each day. For me, there are certain sports that I have never been inclined to try, due to both fear and sanity. Mountaineering is one of them. Put me in an airplane, and I have no problem looking down at the earth. I feel safe in flight, even looking down through the glass bubble bottom of a helicopter's co-pilot seat.

But when it comes to standing on the edge of a cliff, I get wobbly. Once, when I was a twelve-year-old Boy Scout on a camping trip in the Sierras, my entire troop sauntered over and plopped down on the edge of a cliff. They dangled their feet over, even kicking them out and letting them bounce back against the rock, as kids are prone to do. Except me. I stayed thirty feet back from the lip, wanting nothing whatsoever to do with having a vast space between the soles of my shoes and the security of Mother Earth. The passage of time has done nothing to lessen that conviction.

For Gerard Fusil to schedule a mountaineering-oriented Raid, and for me to feel a magical tug to compete in said Raid, was almost like a cruel joke. If I had experienced this crazy drive (Todd Balf, a writer friend, calls his own compulsion to push himself beyond his known limits "the annual urge to do something stupid") toward Borneo, for instance, the only mountaineering would have been the occasional rappel. Same with Madagascar. So as we prepared to enter the autumn months and final Raid preparation, I was acutely aware that I wasn't the man who should be leading us fearlessly through the Andes. We needed an expert. Someone for whom carabiners and a climbing harness were daily wardrobe. A pro who could lead us across a glacier without plunging into a crevasse (or, if one of us fell, could lead a successful rescue), up a mountain without slipping, and down a long rappel without a care.

His name, as Sue told me when I returned her phone call, was Jay Smith. He'd been the chief rigger for the Eco-Challenge, responsible for anchoring the ropes for the 400-foot rappel into Horseshoe Canyon and the 1,200-foot ascent up from the Colorado River afterward.

Jay sent me an autobiography in late August. One look told me we had the right guy. "Jay Smith is recognized as one of the premier mountaineering experts in the United States. A member of the North Face climbing team and a veteran of twenty international expeditions, including climbs in Antarctica, the Himalayas, and Alaska. He is considered America's most experienced Patagonian climber, with six major first ascents in the region, including being the first American to climb all three Torres in the Fitz Roy region."

In addition, Jay had been instructing U.S. Special Forces groups on rock climbing for over ten years, which is how Mike and Jay came to know each other. Even with Mike no longer on active duty, the two still climbed together frequently and were fast friends. It was Mike who asked Jay to be on our team. With that personal request, we went from a team having no mountaineering background whatsoever to a team with one of the best climbers in the world. He had landed in our laps overnight. With him came knowledge and connections, for Jay seemed to know someone at every major mountaineering company. He would be a great asset in securing the needed boots, headlamps, crampons, and other bits of miscellanea.

There was a photo as part of the bio sheet. It was a curious shot, which drew me back to stare at it again and again. Partly because we hadn't met and I was curious about my new teammate's appearance, and partly because there was a certain quality to the picture that I couldn't put my finger on.

The shot was taken in Antarctica. Jay has a huge down jacket on, with the hood pulled up to conceal all but his face and bushy salt-and-pepper mustache. He isn't looking directly into the camera, but out the side of his eyes, as if stealing a glance. As a bio shot it serves its purpose well: The picture is composed perfectly, so that the canary yellow of his parka forces your eyes to zoom toward the photo, then linger on his face. But as a definitive personal portrait—and all bio photos are—it's a mysterious choice. There's an air of elusiveness. He looks like an intensely private individual loathe to be scrutinized, even by the camera.

Interesting, I thought as I took another look, and definitely an in-dividual. One thing that made me proud of our team was its composi-tion. Each of us was a self-starter and free-thinker. No "yes" men. A writer, a freelance TV producer, a kayaker, and a commando. And now a climber. A gen-u-ine mountain climber who'd been up Everest.

Perfect. He would fit right in.

"Welcome aboard," I told Jay when we first spoke. "We're really glad to have you."

"Hey, I just hope I can keep up with you guys," he replied humbly.

CHAPTER 7

Tahoe, Moab, and Mammoth

A tenet of the Raid is that competitors must juggle a real life as they prepare. And preparation means not just physical training, but also raising money. Chasing the Raid dream meant serious juggling. Here's a short list of my ongoing projects from September through November:

1) freelance writing

2) raising money for the Raid

3) securing team equipment for the Raid

4) training for the Raid

5) serving as editor of *CitySports*, a magazine distributed throughout California

6) writing a screenplay with David

7) writing a book about in-line skating

8) acting as a referee for Devin's youth soccer league

I BEGAN each day at 5 AM with coffee and the *Los Angeles Times*. Those were the only moments of real order before the chaos set in. The majority of each day was spent either hunched over my laptop or with a phone glued to my ear. I fit a long run and weight lifting in somewhere. I tried to adhere to a daily regimen of 200 push-ups and sit-ups. Mostly I tried to wade through the list of responsibilities I'd been foolish enough to assume and tried to cram everything else in around them. More than once I finished the day frustrated from the nonstop activity. I would wonder aloud to Calene whether a simple race was worth the trouble. What usually got me back on track was the simple reminder that this was one storm I'd prayed very hard for.

The worst part was I couldn't chop anything from the list.

Freelancing and editing paid the bills. The Raid was taking on a life of its own. The in-line book was due November 30, three days after I planned on leaving for Argentina, which meant it had to be finished early. I couldn't expect David to do all of the screenplay, though I gave that serious thought (and wondered why I'd committed in the first place). And I was so busy that I was spending too little time with Devin and Connor already. Cutting out soccer would have been inconceivable. Day after day I slowly learned an appreciation for the concept of personal limitations. The learning curve was counter to balance, a concept I hold dear. Total commitment has way too much credibility in our society, and leads to nothing more than burnout and empty lives.

I'm a case in point.

The story begins ten years ago, when I lifted words from Bruce Springsteen's "The River" album to propose. I tried to look nonchalant while palming a diamond ring and suddenly feeling vulnerable, as if my intentions were tattooed on my forehead. We were in Laguna Beach—sitting on Laguna Beach, in fact—and, to this day, I kick myself for not getting off my ass and onto bended knee. "Calene, I wear my love without shame, and I'd be proud if you would wear my name. Will you marry me?"

We met while working in a restaurant. It was my last year of college and her last year of graduate school (I fooled around and took about nine years to finish college, but that's a whole other story). The first night we went out together it was with a group of friends to a small club in Laguna. The band was loud. Good loud, but loud. We had to shout back and forth to be heard. I remember looking across the table and thinking, this is the woman I'm gonna marry. It came out of the blue, the clearest, most startling revelation. I had never thought such a thing before in my life, but this woman . . . how could I not love her? She read the front page of the paper, voted her conscience, listened to everything from Billie Holliday to Billy Joel. She taught aerobics five times a week. She was passionate, loving, brutally honest. She was also stubborn, and not satisfied until a problem was talked through, all the way down to the most insignificant detail.

Four months later I proposed. And she, totally surprised, said yes.

Romantic words and trembling knees were, in retrospect, the easy part. Being married was the real work. It took me awhile to get the hang of it. I spent the first few years of married life consumed with my passion for triathlon competition. Every spare minute was spent training. Before work, I rode my bike. At lunch, I ran. After work, I swam. Mix that in with the million hours I worked each week and it's no wonder Devin was six months old before it really hit me that I was a father.

I also realized, wandering into the house one Saturday after eight solid hours of training, that my marriage wasn't all it could be. In fact, it wasn't much. Being away so often meant I was losing touch. Devin didn't know who I was. Calene gave me only blank stares when I rambled on about the wonders of day-long training rides.

As I stood in the doorway that August afternoon, dripping sweat on the tile while wiping chain grease off the inside of my right calf, I realized things had to change. I wasn't training nonstop because I wanted to be a world champion. I was doing it because—for all my alleged romanticism—I was deathly afraid of the closeness and intimacy a strong relationship could bring.

The problem, as I saw it, was one of balance. There was none in my life. I decided then and there to make a radical change in my training habits, and quit triathlons for good a week later. I learned to sit still and to hang out with Calene and Devin, then Connor when he was born in 1992. I came to embrace the concept of balance between mind, body, soul, relationships, and work. Our marriage got stronger, and I came to revel in parenthood. Once I left the corporate world, that sense of balance was reinforced. I was able to spend more time with Calene and the boys, and not so much time focused on working out or just plain working. Funny thing was, life was not only better because of the balance, but I worked more efficiently and productively.

Somehow, and I still can't figure why, I set that synchronicity aside when I decided to compete in the Raid. I began doing too much. Family time suffered. Only when Calene pointed out the arrogance of my refusing to delegate or give up projects, was I able to see what I'd been doing. "You think you can do everything, but you can't," she fumed. "If you want to do the Raid, fine, I'm behind you all the way. Just don't put us second to a race or to your work. It's not fair to me and it's not fair to the kids."

That hurt. Worst part was, she was right.

The talk brought me back to earth. I subsequently made the decision to put several projects aside (screenplay, book), turned equipment procurement over to Sue, and put *CitySports* on the back burner. Our household became a more peaceful, connected place. The stresses of balancing marriage, family, work, and Raid became a huge test of our marriage, but thankfully, it brought us even closer together rather than driving us apart. When things got really crazy and I wasn't sure which way was up, Calene became the voice of love and logic.

It was a voice I came to depend on, because in the last three months before the Raid, the intensity of team training sessions ratcheted upward. There was one for every fall month, each designed to work on specific disciplines. That was far from enough time together, but with the team spread all over California, it was almost impossible to get together more frequently.

The first was in mid-September. We met in Lake Tahoe for a week of horseback riding, long-distance hiking, and kayaking. As a location, few places simulate the Patagonian Andes like the Tahoe area. The elevation is over a mile high. It is alpine, ringed by soaring mountains. The freshwater lake, whipped up each afternoon by stiff winds, is exactly like the vast lakes around the Bariloche starting line.

The five of us, plus team doctor Billy Trolan and alternate Jim Garfield, lounged in Billy's living room on a sunny Monday morning, drinking big mugs of French roast coffee and making idle chit-chat. The horseback riding would come first, then an all-night hike. Tuesday would be kayaking. Wednesday and Thursday would be a nonstop hike from Jay's house in Tahoe Paradise all the way up to Billy's house. If you look at Lake Tahoe on the map, it is roughly the shape of a marquis cut diamond. Our long hike would take us from the bottom of the diamond to the top, a distance of almost fifty-three miles through appropriately named Desolation Wilderness.

There was another face in the room that morning, one I didn't recognize, a friend of Jay's named Robert Finlay. Sunburned, with a Julius Caesar haircut, Robert sometimes worked for Jay's guide company. He hadn't been invited to train with us, but because he was with Jay, who had himself turned out to be a very pleasant guy and not as withdrawn as I'd guessed, he was more than welcome.

The week went even more smoothly than our Saddleback training. Nobody had any problems. Not with altitude, wind, heat, cold, or distance. Jay fit in perfectly, and regaled us with stories about his climbs, particularly one in Alaska where he woke after a night on the wall to find his ropes frozen to the face beneath an inch of new ice.

It was thrilling coming together as a team, marching in a single-file line, helping each other through low points, telling bad jokes to ease the boredom, reminding each other to do the little things like change socks frequently (to prevent blisters) that would make the hike a worthwhile experience instead of brute agony. Toward the end of the fifty-three-miler, when we'd been marching for almost twenty-four hours straight, a sixty-mile-per-hour wind blasted us as we walked a ridgeline beneath a pale full moon. We worked together, encouraging each other with reminders that it was a perfect warm-up for the raging gales of Patagonia. And once again, we ended a training evolution high on ourselves. We were so can't-miss it was incredible. Our team that still had no name was sure to be the first American team to win the Raid Gauloises.

Before catching a flight home, we penciled in dates for the next training session. We decided there would be an optional session in Moab, Utah, in October to work on whitewater canoeing skills. In early November we would meet in Mammoth Lakes for a weekend of ice climbing and last-minute fine-tuning. Other than that, we were all in charge of our own fitness.

The months passed. Things got tense as we counted down the days to our departure. The biggest problem was money: We had none. Though our entry fee was long-since paid, we still needed to come up with travel costs and other miscellaneous gear expenses. That figure was roughly $35,000, and with our departure looming just two months off we had accumulated a grand total of only $2,500. Since I was the one working the phones, the pressure lay squarely on my shoulders.

I began getting phone calls from Jay and Mike, curious about when all the money would start flowing in. At first, they were lighthearted, and I was able to laugh it off with "it's coming, it's coming." But as September became October, they began to get more concerned. Jay told me flat-out that he was going to quit if money didn't start showing up.

He had other plans, he said. He couldn't waste his time devoted to a Raid team that wasn't going to compete. Mike heard about Jay's threat and began saying the same thing. The calls panicked me, because our navigator and lead climber were indispensable. Without them, we simply didn't have the expertise to compete.

If nothing else, I reassured them, I was working night and day to get some money. In fact, the quest for money had consumed me. I was developing sales skills I never knew I had, cold-calling major corporations and asking them to donate to a crazy event not widely known outside Europe. Money began to trickle in, but when the time came for the Moab training session there wasn't enough to foot the bill for everyone. Don called me to say he didn't have enough money to make the trip. He'd quit his job to focus on Raid training, and things were tight.

"Don't worry about it," I told him. "I can't afford to go either." And I couldn't. I was spending too much time raising money for the Raid and not enough time bringing in new writing assignments. With the training evolution already designated as optional, my priorities lay with feeding my family.

In the end, Sue and Mike met Jay at his second home in Moab, a small town on the Utah-Colorado border through which the Colorado River flows. The three of them spent the weekend under the tutelage of a whitewater guide, who showed them how to read good water (the ripples form "happy faces") and troublesome water ("bad faces"). The water was cold and the leaves still on the trees were red and yellow, and the three of them generally had a great time among the striking red-rocked beauty of Moab. At night there was red wine or Coors Light. And conversation. Lots of it, and most of it about Don. Jay and Mike, it turned out, wanted him off the team. They said his inability to make the Moab trip was evidence of his lack of commitment.

It was Sue who broke the news to me, but Jay whom I had to call, to prevent any bad blood. I told him that Don was an asset, reminded him that Don was an original member of the team, and that he was working on bringing in Adidas as a team sponsor. Jay countered by saying that he didn't want to compete on the same team with Don. By the time we hung up, Jay was once again threatening to quit. There was no reason in particular that Jay wanted Don out, other than a desire for more control. A small issue, a nagging grain of sand that grew into an irritant that divided the team.

Every group aligns itself into subgroups sooner or later, and I could see the same happening to my team. Don and I were one group. We talked on the phone frequently, had some of the same friends and possessed an incredible drive to do the Raid. Sue, though she and I talked each day and were very close, was in the middle, receptive to both sides. Jay and Mike were another group, with Robert sniffing around the fringes. As long as we all remained a tight team I didn't mind the divisions, but Jay's disposition toward Don was so negative that I knew it would take fast footwork to shore things up and make us the same tight group that bonded atop that wind-blasted ridge in Tahoe.

Instead of getting better, though, the tension escalated. Lack of money and disenchantment with Don had Jay and Mike threatening to quit at least once a week. As a solution, I suggested that Don and Jay talk on the phone to even out their differences. And though they spoke several times, I began to see that the two would probably never get along. I don't think it was ever anything Don did, it was simply that Jay was much more comfortable with Robert, and wanted to share the Raid experience with him.

By the time Don and I drove to Mammoth on November 10, I knew things were about to come to a head. I prepared him for the worst on the way up. "If it comes down to a vote," I warned him, suddenly aware that I had very little say and was no longer much more than the symbolic head of my own team, "it could get ugly. Be ready."

"MAN, IT'S freezing out here," I shivered, letting the team into the small condo we would share. It was close to midnight, with the temperature hovering just above freezing. Mammoth is a small ski town on the eastern slope of the Sierra, whose most well-known feature is a still-active volcano. I've been going there for ten years to enjoy the mountain trails in summer and the skiing in winter. My memories of the town are almost all fond. Calene and I know the local shops well enough to call the bookstore (the Booky Joint—small, crammed with books, short on attitude) and pizza parlor (Giovanni's, best known for its thick-crust pizza and beautiful Australian waitresses) two of our favorite such establishments anywhere. We almost moved there once, before deciding that we were city people at heart, and would feel isolated in Mammoth, exactly 340 miles from our doorstep in Rancho Santa Margarita but light years away from the convenience of Southern California.

As I opened the door to the condo, though, my mood was far from relaxed. There was bloodletting to be done. We passed through the doorway by region: Don, Sue and I, up from Southern California; Mike, who'd come in from the Bay area. Jay and Billy drove down from Tahoe. Robert Finlay was there too, a fact that both surprised and angered Don.

We assembled, bitched about the cold. I sprawled on the couch, glad to be in Mammoth, but anxious about what was about to transpire. Mike lay on the floor, almost hidden by a pine coffee table. Sue sat upright in a chair, near Billy. Appropriately, Jay and Don and Robert, the three centers of the storm, stood side-by-side against the kitchen table.

No one wanted to bring up the business at hand. We chattered on about this and that, avoiding topics like the team and the Raid. Don remained stone silent, his anxious grin nowhere to be seen. There is normally a softness to Don's features—rounded face, thin layer of fat on top of rippled muscles, perfectly coifed hairstyle—but his appearance was harsh that night. The hair was newly clipped, buzz-cut short. Training had taken the weight off his face. The posture was rigid. Eyes narrow. Lips pursed.

None of us consciously knew it as we bantered about nothing, but the sound we needed to hear was Don's voice. That would be our signal. "Folks," he finally announced after midnight. His voice was deep but shaky, and I think he'd needed his hour of silence to get his courage up. "Before we go on I think there's something we need to talk about."

For the next ten minutes Don laid out in detail the reasons why he should be on the team: kayaking skills, overall fitness, time invested, original member, actively pursuing sponsors. He spoke softly, but there was restrained anger in every word. It was the helpless rage that comes from being misunderstood. "That's it. Anyone have anything they'd like to say?" he concluded.

Nobody spoke, which didn't surprise me. I'd been getting phone calls all week from Jay, Mike, and Sue, each one listing reasons why Don didn't belong. My response was always to tell them to call Don and confront him on the issues, but no one ever did. That they would continue the silence in Mammoth wasn't right, though. And now it was my turn to be the voice that people were waiting to hear. I cleared my throat and spoke. "OK," I began, "let's talk about this. Mike, you've had a lot to say. Sue. You too, Jay. Let's get this out in the open."

It got bloody after that. One by one, team members ticked off a litany of Don's transgressions. Mike thought Don's choice of in-line skating as a favorite training technique was too unconventional. Sue bridled that Don once called her "princess." Jay had ordered a kayak but Don forgot to place the order with the factory.

What was certain as the tempo escalated was that Don was out. Too much hostility was being released for the discussion to reenter the realm of cathartic. Don knew it. I knew it. The team knew it.

The discussion went on for almost an hour. I let the team talk itself out, with Don answering in kind. Finally, Don, Robert, and Billy stepped outside into the freezing air to give the four principals time to vote. When they came back fifteen minutes later, it was my job as captain to tell Don that the vote had been three to one against him. After six months as a member of my Raid team, he was off. He could still be the alternate, I said. He could still make the trip and hang out with us in Argentina. "If we ever get the money . . . ," I added, trying to soften the blow by implying that none of us might go.

"Nope." Don grabbed his gear and stepped back out into the night. It was almost two. "I'll see you guys later. I can't be sticking around here tonight." I walked Don out to his car. We shook hands. As Don got into his truck to drive back home, I was struck by a thought. "Do you think that if I wasn't the one raising the money, that I'd be the one being fired instead?"

Don had a bittersweet smile on his face. "You know it, buddy."

Five minutes later it was my responsibility to welcome Robert Finlay aboard the team. It was awful, almost a feeling of betrayal. Yet oddly, I felt more peaceful than I had in weeks. Without Don we were suddenly conflict-free. The petty phone calls about his alleged inferiorities would cease. And ironically, I soon got along with Robert best of all. The product of a wealthy Southern California family, he'd graduated from West Point and spent eight years as an Army Ranger. Things went wrong somewhere along the line. He went from being one of the Army's best, invited to White House functions, to leaving the military. He chose to work as an ironworker, strangely enough, providing structural integrity for bridges and skyscrapers. He did that only six months out of the year. The other six were spent in a world he controlled, rock climbing in places like Joshua Tree, miles out in the California desert, and in Idaho. For fun, Robert liked solitary forced marches across the desert during the blistering heat of summer.

"I got bitten by a scorpion once," he'd told me. I wasn't surprised. It also didn't surprise me that Robert had survived, because his body was wiry and taut, trained for the battles he created for himself. He was so taken with confronting hardship that I wouldn't have been surprised if he had actively scoured the desert floor for a scorpion, then offered it his arm. To test his nerve, Robert had already pierced his left nipple (twice—and not the areola, but the nipple itself), and his scrotum (also twice). He described the scrotum procedure: "I did it the first time for a girlfriend. When they pierced me I wet myself and passed out. I could see a white light and it felt like I was having a near-death experience. But I took that one out after she broke up with me."

"But you still have it in."

"Yeah. I kinda missed having it, so I got it pierced again."

"Did it hurt as badly the second time?"

"Oh, yeah."

I related best to the West Point grad still lurking within Robert, a student of military history who thrilled at discussing the lives of great men and their battles. We found common ground discussing the ancient Greeks and Persians and their assorted wars. Alexander the Great was of special significance. My minor in college was history, and I can still reel off Alexander's accomplishments, as well as those of his father, Philip II of Macedon. But Robert was so far beyond me. Not only did he know of Alexander and Philip, but had even visited Alexander's battlefields, some as far away as the Indus River in what is now Pakistan, the farthest reach of Alexander's campaign for world conquest. He would relate in West Point detail why Alexander was successful early in his quest for world domination, and also why he ultimately failed. Robert's knowledge was so vast that I became merely a rapt listener.

It was a relief talking to someone on the team about something other than the Raid. I had nothing in common with Jay or Mike. When I talked with Robert I never knew whether I would get the rebellious body piercer or the introspective West Pointer, but at least our conversations ventured beyond the superficial. I was beginning to feel like an outsider on the team. Talking history with Robert made the connection true again.

When we went ice climbing the day after Don's departure there was a new tone to the team. We were lighter, more professional. The vote had set a precedent. Now we were the adventure racing equivalent of the New York Yankees, a team of free agents with little in common.

Instead of one guy making decisions, we were five individuals, each with a vote. My only task was to raise money and coordinate, which sounded important in the weeks before the race, but would mean absolutely nothing during the Raid itself. I began to worry that I might not be able to hold the group together as a single unit during the Raid. Worse, I began to wonder if I might somehow become expendable. What if the Jay/Robert/Mike alignment, which was solid, wanted to make another change, and what if that change was me? The pragmatism of it all struck me like an ice pick between the eyes as we hiked from an empty Coldwater Campground up past Emerald Lake to the ice field.

At times of insecurity and inferiority I think it's best to deal from a position of strength. This is the time to showcase a skill, or make a convincing argument. Ice climbing, unfortunately, was not the place for me to do such a thing.

"Now when you hold your ice axe," Jay began when we reached the ice field, wielding an ice axe in his left hand, "you want to grasp it like this, towards the base, so you can get greater leverage when you swing it into the ice." An ice axe is about two feet long, with a rubberized grip and a sharpened steel point like the business end of a pickax.

"When you walk on crampons, you want to walk like this," and now Jay was walking up a steep, icy slope. Jay thudded each step down hard to ensure maximum purchase. He walked up ten meters, then down ten meters. Crampons have sharp spikes on the bottom that dig into ice, and two thin steel points extending straight out in front of the toe. These are to be used in climbing, which is scary when you consider that each is no greater in length and width then the sharpened point of a pencil. "OK, now you guys try it."

I looked up at the ice field. From where I stood at the base, it sloped steeply upward to vertical, where it rose straight up for 100 meters to a rocky spine. The blue-gray ice was in the morning shadows, which only added to its sinister appearance. Standing at the base, I felt like a dope in my brand new crampons, holding an ice axe from which I'd just removed the price tag. Ice climbing is not for clumsy, scared people like me, it is for people with acrobatic grace and balls of stone. I wondered why I was there, then looked at the spine so high above and prayed that we did not have to climb up there.

So, of course, we did. At first, we were all scared. Sue, Robert, and Mike looked as awkward as I did, thumping around in crampons, wielding ice axes like spastics. But when we began going upward they found their motor skills anew, while I was derelict, too chicken to proceed up the vertical section. Jay, who was having such fun that he climbed all the way to the top and back down before I really got motivated to do much of anything, eyed me curiously. The others were all high above, pressed to the ice, swinging ice axes to secure new holds.

"You OK, Marty?"

"I, uh, I'm fine. I'm just not all that comfortable with going up there."

"Maybe you should just stay down here and practice then."

"Right. Good idea." And it was a good idea. Only problem was that Sue, Robert, and Mike were 200 feet above me, climbing like pros. Basically, I was being a wimp. Sue and the others were being brave. No two ways about it, if I was going to be able to hold my head high whenever future discussions turned to ice climbing, I would have to put my well-founded fears aside and climb. Never mind that we weren't roped in, and that a fall would most certainly be fatal, I had to climb. I squared off and looked straight up the ice. I prayed. I grasped my ice axe. I began climbing.

Ten minutes later I'd gone just fifty yards, but I was solidly on vertical and not liking it one bit. The routine for upward movement was a continual shifting of weight from one point of contact with the ice to another: ice axe, crampon, crampon. Only a half-inch portion of each extended into the ice at any one time. I never looked up or down. My world consisted of the pockmarked ice in front of me. Nothing else mattered. Swing, step, step, swing, step, step, swing, step, step. I tried not to think about going down. The very idea made me want to wet my pants. I just focused on going up. Swing, step, step. Swing, step, step.

Sue passed me on her way back down. I snuck a peek and was relieved to notice that the task was no easier for her. Sue's good at that, I reminded myself. She never likes to look weak. Sue's whole athletic persona is built around never showing weakness. So whereas I might be able to look up and note aloud that something scares me or seems very tough, Sue doesn't grant herself that luxury. The way I was able to tell when Sue was scared or tired was that she just stopped talking. When Sue was strong and unafraid, she chattered a mile a minute. When life got bad, she shut up until the ordeal was past.

Against long odds I reached the summit. With my free hand, I snagged a chip of rock and stuffed it in my pocket (it is on my desk before me as I write). Then, I made the conscious effort to calm myself. It was taking every last bit of energy within me to suppress my fear that I was about to die. Fear like that can be paralyzing. I was in a totally self-sufficient position unable to afford the luxury of paralysis by fear. Either I climbed the wall and came back down in one piece, or I climbed the wall and freaked out—which was what I was doing, and which did me no good whatsoever because nobody was capable of saving me. It wasn't as if Jay could just throw me across his back and carry me back down the ice. No, either I climbed and descended by myself or I freaked out and fell to my death because I was incapable of controlling fear. My choice.

Everyone else was waiting for me back at the bottom. I took a deep breath, then made my only real mistake of the day: I looked down. What I saw was the tiniest tip of each crampon—a mere whit of steel sticking into the ice, holding me to the wall. And space. That was all. I was more off the wall than on, my fate entirely in the hands of modern metallurgy. Should one of those tips break or even bend, I was a dead man.

A surge of adrenaline shot through me, making my heart beat too fast and my throat constrict. If I had needed to speak right then, I would have made some sort of high-pitched noise, but nothing intelligible. I turned back to focus on the ice. My eyes drilled a hole in the patch six inches in front of my face. I remember it now, sun-dimpled and gray. Hardly pristine ice. I took deep breaths. I prayed some more. I thought of my family. And then, slowly, very slowly, I climbed back down, staring straight forward the entire time.

I GOT back from Mammoth on a Sunday night. Inexplicably, the phone began ringing the moment I stepped into the office Monday morning. North Face wanted to write us a sponsorship check. Adidas wanted to write us a check. Dockers, most substantially, wanted to come on as title sponsor. For that, they were prepared to write a very big check. Keith Bruce of Foote, Cone and Belding in San Francisco brokered the Dockers deal, and we spent most of Monday and Tuesday hammering out details. Bruce had been responsible for hooking up Gatorade with the Ironman Triathlon. He thought, as I did, that the Raid would be the '90s version of the Ironman, the next big thing for endurance athletes the world over. After months of trying to convince big companies of that, it was a relief when someone else saw my point of view. Bruce then convinced Robert Hanson and Heidi Oestrike of Dockers that sponsoring a Raid Gauloises team was just about the smartest sports marketing move they could possibly make.

　　Thus, Team Dockers was born. The money to make it happen came November 21, just six days before we left for the Raid. When I added up the contributions of Dockers, North Face, Adidas, and smaller companies like PowerBar and Cytomax, I wasn't surprised to find that we had just enough money to go. Not too much. Not too little. But just enough.

Gerard Fusil

Don Baker, Team American Pride tryout,
Los Angeles, 1994

Bruce Schliemann, Raid Gauloises, Patagonia, 1995

Raid Gauloises,
Patagonia, 1995

Pat Harwood,
Raid Gauloises,
Patagonia, 1995

Raid Gauloises, Patagonia, 1995

Raid Gauloises, Patagonia, 1995

Eco-Challenge, British Columbia, 1996

Raid Gauloises, Lesotho, 1997

Jim Garfield, Raid Gauloises, Lesotho, 1997

David Tracey and friend, Raid Gauloises, Lesotho, 1997

Eco-Challenge, Australia, 1997

Cathy Sassin-Smith, Raid Gauloises,
Lesotho, 1997

TRACY ST. JOHN

Juliette Oomer, Raid Gauloises,
Lesotho, 1997

Eco-Challenge, Australia, 1997

CHAPTER 8

The Streets of Bariloche

Patagonia, 1995

"Ain't no Fusil gonna greet me,

  it's just you and I my team,

  my clothes don't fit me no more,

  I'd walk a million miles just to finish this thing."

      —Unofficial Raid anthem, "The Streets of Bariloche"

      (sung to the tune of "Streets of Philadelphia")

BARILOCHE IS a German/Italian/Swiss town that somehow transplanted itself to Argentina in the days after World War II, when Bariloche had no airport and was so far across the barren Pampas from Buenos Aires that authorities didn't trouble rousting the new arrivals with niggling immigration questions like previous associations with known fascist regimes. The decor as you walk the main streets is Swiss chalet, all lacquered wood beams and mottled brick. The coffee is thick, black, and bitter enough that it's best taken with at least a dollop of sugar. Local fare is invariably the simple cheese and green olive pizza; or plump, spicy sausage, washed down with some form of black beer. Rich, delicate pastry is dessert. Spanish has remained the prevalent language, but it's spoken with Old World civility. The California kitchen Spanish I'd learned in the restaurant business went largely understood but sounded gruff in comparison.

Which is a very roundabout way of saying Patagonia was the Raid location I'd been waiting three years for. Not Antananarivo, where the foul smell of open sewers wafted into restaurants. Not Kuching, where the ocean was too polluted with raw sewage to swim. Bariloche was

European civilization at its finest. Best part was, we could see the likely Raid course every time we stepped outside. The Andes ring Bariloche, and every time I looked at them I had that awful premonition I would possibly fall from them.

The Hotel Panamericano was twenty-two kilometers up Lago Nahuel Huapi's perimeter from the center of town. I liked it, especially the way that our balcony looked out onto the lake. I spent a lot of time out there reading and watching the wind push the clouds across the whitecapped lake. Patagonia was just entering into spring and the weather was still unpredictable—cold one moment, balmy the next. I'd sit out there in a down jacket after the sun went down, acclimating to the snap of cold against my cheeks after training so long in the California sun.

I wasn't nervous about the race, but I wasn't in a hurry for it to happen, either. And while my teammates slept inside, I sat on the balcony, trying to appreciate the beauty of Patagonia without being intimidated by it.

Every single inch of floor space in our hotel rooms was covered with equipment and food as we readied for the race. We puttered with our packs for hours, trying to find the best way of merging the sharp points of crampons and ice axes inside a pack with boots, foul weather gear, and food without sacrificing waterproof integrity or adding unwanted weight. North Face had specially designed lightweight packs for us. Even so, Fusil's quest to give the Raid an expeditionary flair meant a mandatory gear list a mile long and my pack weighed in at a startling fifty-five pounds, even after whittling down to no optional gear whatsoever.

There was too much work to be done to slip away often, but when I could I made my way two kilometers up the road to the Hotel Temenquel, headquarters for Raid officials and journalists. Even five minutes in the presence of Sean, David, Antoine, and Aris, the awesomely talented Italian photographer, was enough to make me laugh so much that all my anxieties about the Raid disappeared. There were new faces, too: Tony DiZinno, my Disneyland photographer, and Adrian "The Mad Argentinian," who had a thick Spanish accent and was born in Buenos Aires, yet lived in Sydney. Laughter was never in short supply with that group and conversation never lagged.

Those times, however, were few, as each day was filled from dawn to dusk with team preparations. I wrote in my journal two days after our arrival:

"Should have written sooner but I have had no time. This Raid thing has consumed both me and the team, eating up days and nights until we forget the expensive lunches here at the Hotel Panamericano and the late hour. We sort gear, label bags, sew patches (on our team uniforms), bag food, or otherwise labor incessantly to reassure ourselves that we will not run out of anything or be unduly put out during the Raid, which is perhaps the biggest example of being put out on the planet."

The last bit of overstatement seems ludicrous in retrospect, but is a good reflection of our prerace mindset. The Raid was the most important thing in the world to us. With the problems of money, team financing, and travel finally behind us, Team Dockers was fixated on nothing but the race. Tension was high in our little suite of rooms at the Panamericano (suite being something of a misnomer, since our lacquered pine–paneled, single bed, three-room cluster in the cinder-block hotel felt like a well-appointed college dorm), but we were all walking on eggshells, trying to get along.

An example of the unspoken tension: Jay had long been sponsored by North Face, and lobbied hard for our team to be called Team North Face. One feature of North Face products (indeed, of any high-quality outdoor wear) is synthetic fabric. A major benefit of synthetics is their ability to dry quickly and wick moisture away from the skin. North Face would be the gear we would compete in.

Dockers had paid to be title sponsor, however. A basic tenet of their advertising is all-natural fabrics, specifically cotton. Which is why we wore their clothing as casual prerace wear. All except Jay. In addition to boycotting Dockers, he wore buttons proclaiming his allegiance to North Face: "Cotton Kills" and "See No Weevil," that were part of a North Face ad campaign. Like I said, little things, and unspoken, but they added up.

Our forced camaraderie was transparent, however. "You know, dude," David pointed out after touring the clutter and confusion of our suite, "the attitude around here is that you guys hate each other."

I said nothing, hoping he was wrong. We didn't hate each other,

I swore to myself, he just didn't understand us. There would be no reunion one year hence, but we certainly bore no malice toward each other. We were just intense, all of us, putting on our game faces a little differently than other teams. But hatred? No.

"I think one of two things is going to happen," David went on. "Either you guys are going to take all this incredible negative energy and turn it into some kind of weird competitive fire. Or . . . "

"Or what?"

"Or you're going to self-destruct and kill each other."

I laughed. David just didn't understand: Team Dockers was going to win.

My journalistic friends all were behind the crazy idea that one of them would actually compete. They made jokes about all the helicopter rides and late nights I'd miss, but each one of them—except Antoine, who spoke more often with a nod or a raised eyebrow than a word—said out loud that they were behind me all the way. "You look really fit. I'm happy for you that this has all come together," Sean informed me in a moment of seriousness as I gave him a tour of our suite. I was about to say something warmhearted in return, but as the two of us were standing there, Robert picked that moment to step out of the shower and show us all his scrotum ring.

"THIS PLACE looks like the Reichstag," Billy Trolan exclaimed just loud enough for the German concierge to overhear. Along with all the other teams, we were filing into the Hotel Llao Llao for the prerace briefing. The hotel was daunting, a German hunting lodge expanded a hundred-fold, then crammed with amenities like fine crystal, high tea, and very expensive-looking artwork on the walls. "Look at the art— pre-World War II German. Can you believe that?" Billy rambled on. I wanted to—the thought that we had stumbled into a rogue Nazi hide-away was compelling in a very *Twilight Zone* sort of way—but I didn't know enough about art to agree or call Billy's bluff. I chose to believe him, if for no other reason than the fact that the prerace briefing was sending an adrenaline rush through me like none I'd ever felt before. To see our team in their uniforms—flat-front khaki pants, hiking boots, denim Dockers shirts festooned with team number 77, Raid logo, and team insignia—for the first time, as well as seeing the other fifty teams in their finery after days of puttering around in T-shirts and jeans was most motivating.

"I wish we could start the damn race right now," I told Billy, not responding to his Nazi suspicions. "Man, am I pumped."

And that was before we entered the actual briefing room. In Borneo, the briefing had been in a small, airless room. In Madagascar, a cramped auditorium. For Patagonia, though, Fusil pulled out all the stops. The briefing room was the hotel ballroom, a cavernous place big enough for a thousand swirling, waltzing Nazis. The ceiling was fifty feet high. Windows on one wall reached all the way up there from the floor, showing off Lago Nahuel Huapi and a jagged peak known as Cerro Lopez. The room was either brand-new or exquisitely maintained, as nothing in its appearance suggested that dirt or dust had ever smudged the beautiful pine walls.

Amid the hustle-bustle of 250 competitors, 100 journalists, 100 Raid staffers, and assorted others, we took our seats. The non-French speakers slipped on headphones to hear a translation of what Fusil would have to say. Course maps were passed out for the first time. I carried my journal with me:

"3:08 PM. In the briefing room. More stuff to think about as we just received course maps and the guide book. Looks like lots of paddling and portaging. Some climbing and walking. A lot of horseback riding. Feel nervous, happy, ready.

"I am ready. I look out at the blue waters of the lake in front of our hotel, and think of Lake Tahoe, then feel assured that kayaking on it will be nothing new to me. I smell the moist, cold air, laced with the smell of green grass, and think of Marquette, Michigan, and get strong. I see the peaks across the lake—snowcapped, glistening, stunningly gorgeous—and am taken back to the summer I worked in Jackson Hole. Am I ready for this Raid? Without a doubt."

Fusil began speaking at 3:15. He went over the course in detail. Day One would be a kayak prologue, twenty kilometers. Day Two would be the start of the Raid proper. In order, we would kayak, mountaineer, canoe and portage, ride horseback, canoe, then climb and rappel. "This will be most difficult," he warned. "There will be falling rocks on the mountains, severe wind and cold at night, and a more strenuous Raid than you have imagined. Take every precaution."

I was listening and studying a small pocket map at the same time. Neither the kayaking nor mountaineering looked long. But for reasons of safety (and to divide the field), Fusil had mandated a "door" atop 8,000-foot Cerro Lopez, which we would climb immediately after kayaking fifty kilometers across Nahuel Huapi. Teams that did not make it to the summit of Lopez by 9 PM on the Raid's second day would be forced to stop for the night. The "door," in other words, would close. Those teams that summitted before then would find the door open, and would be allowed to continue through the night. In effect, they would gain at least a six-hour lead. Kayaking was our weakest event, but we would always have to be aware that we couldn't afford to lag too far behind. When things got tough during the long hours of kayaking through three-foot swells and thirty-knot winds—when our forearms and shoulders burned from effort and the urge to take a break grew strong—we would need images of that door slamming and Raid victory slipping away to propel us forward.

From then on, the race looked like it was all about perseverance. The canoeing was a long grind down the swollen Rio Manso, laced with twenty-kilometer portages where we would have to deflate our portable canoes, roll them up, and lash them to our backs. Each canoe weighed sixty-five pounds, a weight we would carry in addition to our normal packs.

Horseback riding was next, but Fusil mandated that teams treat their horses with care. No galloping would be permitted, only walking. He stressed that this would not be a time to pass other teams, but to rest and not make a stupid compass mistake that might set you back.

The final canoeing and climbing sections were short, designed to be all-out efforts. The final push was a 500-meter rappel into the finish area. In all the course was 400 miles long. Nobody was expected to finish in less than nine days.

The team commandeered the empty dining room at the Panamericano after dinner. We spent until midnight poring over our maps, drinking thick, black coffee. In the morning we would leave for Villa la Angostura, site of the start, about a two-hour drive north. But we were more concerned with maps than sleep, trying to figure out a winning strategy through the mountains. I made a last note to myself before closing my journal: "We must try to make things happen on the mountaineering phase. It's our strength, and though I think we will be tough, we must attack there."

It would prove prophetic. Our time in the mountains would be one attack after another.

THE RAID began on a Sunday. One-hundred and forty-seven bright red kayaks departed en masse from a gravel beach north of Villa la Angostura. Forty-nine teams from thirteen countries were entered. There were seven from the US, the most ever. The scene was frenzied, with boats and paddles and rudders colliding. It was a literal clash of cultures, with a multilingual screech of profanities to match.

French teams InterSport, Coflexip, and Hewlett-Packard emerged as leaders out of the tangle. Team Dockers was twenty-first.

We finished the kayaking at 4 PM on Day Two and began the mad dash upward to the "door." We climbed at breakneck pace to the summit, a beastly 8,000 feet away—legs on fire, lungs heaving, and me not allowing myself to look down while scaling sections that dropped thousands of feet into the lake. This was the toughest thing I'd ever done in my life. Forget the marathons and triathlons. Part of me thrilled at the wonder of overcoming both a fear of heights and prerace jitters about being a Raid competitor. Another reminded me that it was an awful, punishing climb. I wouldn't care to do it again.

Only six teams made it through the door that night. Team Dockers wasn't one of them. Bitterly disappointed, the five of us camped below the summit, an enclave of rocks and scrub protecting us from the raging wind but not from the freezing temperatures. Fully dressed, we shivered in our lightweight sleeping bags and waited for dawn. Sue, in the throes of altitude sickness and severe dehydration, threw up all night. When we set out again at four AM, her movements were feeble. Half-delirious, using a free hand to slip stomach-friendly Gummi Bears in her mouth to get a jolt of energy, she was petrifying to watch as we snaked up the knife-edge ridge to the summit. One side fell thousands of feet into Nahuel Huapi. The other fell a mere 100 feet onto a snowfield.

The Raid, I was finding, is like that: a continual process of over-coming. Each moment of each day is lived with incredible intensity. There are extremes of pain and exhaustion. Something as simple as putting one foot in front of the other for hours on end becomes a major accomplishment. A competitor told me that in Borneo the emphasis on moving forward—of being positive—made it impossible to think of something as heretical as quitting. "You can't," he said. "You just put one foot in front of the other until you finish." This was the mindset of Team Dockers on Day Three. Quitting wasn't an option; only forward progress. We didn't make the door, but we muddled on, just twelve hours off the lead in seventeenth place. The Raid is such a long race that anything can happen. "They've gotta sleep sometime," Mike reminded us, referring to the lead teams. With that in mind, we moved as swiftly as Sue's deteriorating condition allowed. As we worked to make up ground, the "wonders" of nature became adversaries instead of merely beautiful backdrops. The once-in-a-lifetime splendor of standing atop Cerro Lopez as the sun rises is not awe-inspiring if you must descend that peak (sliding at breakneck speed down a snowfield) and climb two others before noon, all the while haunted by the specter of 11,600-foot Mont Tronador, which must be summitted the next day. Likewise, there was nothing stunning about the cliff-lined shore of Nahuel Huapi stretching over the horizon once I realized we had to kayak the entire length of that coast. And while I finally appreciated Patagonia's beauty after my Raid ended, during the race I saw nothing but suffering in those summits plumed with snow and gray shale. Thetumbling mountain streams, so clear and swift from record snowfall, held not a trace of allure beyond their ability to refill water bottles. And more often, they were an obstacle.

The inevitable finally happened. After three days and nights of her body rejecting all food and water, Sue was forced to abandon the race. We all knew it was coming. In fact, it had become an unspoken source of tension because it would mean the end of our team at the 1995 Raid Gauloises. The instant the helicopter settled to the ground and Sue stepped aboard, Team Dockers was out. Though the four of us would be allowed to go on without her, our finish would be unofficial.

Mike, Jay, Robert, and I went on, but the disappointment had fractured us. We spent the morning of Day Four trekking up a near-vertical snowfield, then had a bitter argument at the summit. After all the preparation and training, to no longer be in the running was a shock. We raged back and forth about each other's faults and weaknesses. The words we screamed were crazy, fueled by frustration and fatigue, then whisked off on the Patagonian winds a second after being uttered. A dozen other teams were at the summit. They crouched behind rocks to cheat the wind, peering out to watch us battle, seeing firsthand what the Raid did to teams.

What began in Moab and continued in Mammoth finally concluded in Patagonia: Team Dockers destroyed itself.

When we finally shut up, calmed down, and shouldered our packs again, we were still too angry to speak. We walked 10 meters apart, each in his own universe. It was a good example why, more than the physical and mental aspects, the team dynamic of the Raid is what makes it a true test of character. Getting along with four people for more than a week is a chore under normal circumstances, but almost impossible when you're cold, tired, wet, hungry, and miserable.

Our split might have healed long enough to get us through the race, but things took a turn for the worse. As we picked our way through a field of unstable shale on a steep descent, I stepped . . . wrong. And just like that, my race was over. After hobbling three miles down the mountain to a checkpoint where I knew there was a doctor, I got the diagnosis: a strained medial collateral ligament.

Gerard Fusil himself helped me to the helicopter, the same one that had borne Sue just hours before. As the helicopter lifted from the ground I saw Jay, Robert, and Mike moving forward without me. I knew why those Germans on Madagascar were so saddened. It wasn't that their race had come to an end. In fact, it had nothing to do with racing, or even competition. They were sad because the Raid is a miserable, painful process that demands personal excellence at all times. The conditions are so severe that you have no choice but to comply. Touching excellence is uplifting and addictive in a way that no drug can ever be. It is the reward that lies beyond the comfort zone and to be ripped from that by fate is grievous.

My injury, which healed within days, seemed slight compared with that of the French woman whose foot was broken by a falling rock. Mike Sawyer of the American Team Odyssey had his right hand crushed by shale. Still, nobody died.

As I prepared to fly home, Fusil asked me, "Will you be coming back next year?"

I thought for a moment of being cold, tired, hungry, and wet. I thought of the heights, of the epic team argument, of bones crushed and knees torn in the blink of an eye. But mostly, I thought of how devastated I was after my Raid came to an end. Did I really want to come back again and suffer? Were my midrace moments of life outside the comfort zone really worth another year of training?

"Of course," I answered, meeting his gaze. The answer had come in a flash. "Of course."

CHAPTER 9

What It Feels Like To Quit the Raid

The flight in the blue-and-white medevac helicopter was stunning, a bird's-eye view of the soaring mountains and valleys I'd been doing battle with. It reminded me of Yosemite Valley, all gray cliffs and pine forests, with waterfalls cascading randomly everywhere the eye looked. I saw only beauty, and felt not a trace of fear.

WHEN THE helicopter set down at the assistance point, I was carried to a small hospital, where doctors prescribed rest and anti-inflammatory drugs. By coincidence, all of my journalist friends—David, Tony, and Sean among them—had been at CP8, the spot where I had abandoned. Their supportive banter and bad jokes made the situation more bearable. Now it was Antoine who made his way into the room where I was lying, a cigarette dangling from one corner of his mouth and eyes squinting from the smoke. I felt too low even to acknowledge him as he looked at my swollen knee, puffing away with a wry, detached look on his face. He asked the doctor a few questions in French. The doctor responded in French, gesturing toward my knee with his index finger.

When the doctor finished, Antoine came close and extended his hand. I shook it. "Welcome back, Martin Dugard. I am glad you are safe. Now," and here he leaned forward to flash the first sincere look I'd ever seen from Antoine, "you are on my team again."

How does it feel to quit the Raid Gauloises? Strangely nurturing.

PART III

Doing It Right

CHAPTER 10

Moby Raid

"We rejoice in our sufferings, because we know that suffering produces perseverance; perseverance, character; and character, hope. And hope does not disappoint us."

—Romans 5: 3–4

I wrote in my journal as I prepared to leave Argentina a week later. I was in the Bariloche airport, a small one-plane facility where jets land, unload, refuel, then leave again immediately. There's no insulation, so when a plane pulls up to the terminal, everyone in the airport knows it because the low whine of idling jet engines is the sole sound. Everyone, that is, except me.

"THIS TRIP gets more wacky by the day. Moments ago, after waiting three full hours for my flight to Buenos Aires, I missed it. I was so engrossed in writing down my Raid recollections that I missed my boarding call. The small, wood-paneled (pine, of course) terminal was filled with people and I mistakenly thought we were all on the same flight. It was only when I heard the engines rev and still saw a crowded terminal that I realized my plane was not only fully boarded, but leaving without me."

I ran frantically to the nearest official, who happened to be not only an Argentine policeman, but the only English-speaking individual on the airport staff. I told him my plight—quickly. He sprang into action. He snatched up a walkie-talkie and called the control tower, asking if they would stop the plane, which by now was almost all the way out to the runway. When that failed, he made sure there was a seat for me on the 6:55 to Buenos Aires. Nice man.

When I left the medical facility after being airlifted off the course,

I wandered through the assistance area to Team Dockers area. The assistance point lay in a verdant meadow ringed by horse pastures. Brightly colored dome tents and four-wheel-drive vehicles crowded a corner of the meadow, forming a Raid shanty town of assistance teams waiting for their Raiders to arrive. The Andes loomed above, particularly Mont Tronador, which people took to calling The Tronador, then just Tronador.

After taking three liters of IV solution the morning she was airlifted out, Sue was up and around. She and Dick were inseparable, making the sort of cute jokes newlyweds make, which they were in some ways, having spent so little of their married life in the same place at the same time. Their bad jokes were fun to hear, especially after seeing Sue in such agony during the race.

Billy Trolan gave me a shot of Toradol for the infections on my hands and tendinitis in my forearms, and a nameless sleeping pill because I was overtired and couldn't sleep. Both of those combined brilliantly with my French anti-inflammatory medicine to knock me out until early evening. When I awoke I was alone on an air mattress in our big yellow North Face dome. My knee was stiff, and a dull throb of regret filled me. I retraced the race in my head, trying to see where I'd gone wrong, and why the team had split so decisively even before the Raid began.

I cursed myself for losing sight of my original goal, which was to complete the Raid at all costs and have a great adventure in the meantime. I'd lost that focus when I'd begun thinking too much about winning. Other teams sang and laughed and helped each other, but we'd done nothing of the sort. When it came right down to it, we were never friends. I was surprised at the way my teammates acted, but I shouldn't have been. Jay came aboard to be the lead climber, and he had performed that function perfectly. Mike was the navigator, and we hadn't gotten lost once. Same with Robert, the backup navigator. But the Raid is a race run on emotion, and a purely functional squad lacks the necessary caring and chemistry. I didn't know that beforehand, and paid the price.

Team aside, my failure had humbled me. I lay on that air mattress for hours after I woke up, staring at the curved yellow ceiling, trying to change what had happened. But I couldn't. The adventure gone wrong was my fault alone, and I was haunted by the thought.

The team came in two days later. Jay apologized for all that had happened. It helped some of the anger to evaporate and made me feel less tormented for a time. When they left to start the canoeing leg I limped out to watch them go. They paddled from the shore into the Rio Manso's emerald current, all three plus gear piled into one olive inflatable canoe.

Journal—December 10, 1995:

> *Sunny afternoon in Patagonia. At canoe finish/horseback start with David, Sean, and Yaro Velez from NBC. Talk about the ozone hole and other inanities while tanning and smearing Argentine moisturizer ("Diazul: Leche de Epinos") on our faces. The team is not yet done with the canoe, which they should have finished two hours ago. They must be tired.*
>
> *Since my Raid has ended I've rafted the Rio Manso and taken press trips and gotten away from the whole team environment. But I'm depressed, I'll admit it. I wish the team had hung together and all that, but mostly I am dazzled at how quickly the fracture occurred—in the race's first hour. I should have seen it coming and now I feel like a fool.*

SLOWLY I slipped from competitor back to journalist. The consuming exertion of rafting was a great help. When most people think of whitewater, they think of bobbing pell-mell through rapids, but it's actually much more physical and cerebral. The physical part is for those doing the paddling. They perch on the inflatable sides of the boat, angling their bodies so that their feet are wedged inside the raft itself, while the upper body hangs out over the river and paddles. Arms and back and abs and shoulders stroke powerfully—hopefully, in synch.

I'm a paddler. I lack the knowledge of rivers necessary to be a good helmsman, which is the truly cerebral aspect of rafting. The helmsman steers the boat from the back, calling out directions to the paddlers in order to keep the boat pointed into the current (the trick in running rapids is to keep the boat headed in the exact same direction the most powerful section of current is headed). "Back paddle" means paddle backward. "Forward paddle" means forward, and so on. When directions are barked improperly or misunderstood due to the roar of rapids, the results can mean disaster: rafts wrapped around boulders, flipped over, spun sideways and out of control. Worst-case scenario for rafting is that people drown, held under by the pummeling force of raging water. Which is why total concentration on the task at hand is crucial. The best boats have a synergy between helmsman and paddlers, as the latter learn to read the current and anticipate instructions. The process is consuming.

And though such excursions helped put the bitterness behind me, it wasn't until one late night that everything came into perspective. There was a chill in the air, a bite that touched bone. David and I were hanging out with Antoine, near a campfire that also doubled as a checkpoint. Antoine was drinking J&B. Another Frenchman, this one more heavyset than Antoine and much more expressive, had been nipping at the bottle for hours and was yodeling loudly into the night. He was an accomplished yodeler, and a crowd of journos and Raid officials were gathered around the fire to urge him on. With every nip he would yodel louder, the sound coming from high in his throat then traveling far down the tranquil valley toward Bariloche, sixty miles away.

Soon a new face appeared, trying to work his way through the crowd to the campfire. He was tall and had red hair. A competitor, not a journalist. I recognized him as Stanislaw Wyganowski, captain of the Polish team. They were in last place. The entire crowd suddenly went still and turned toward him. "Is this the checkpoint?" he asked politely in English.

"What?" It was the yodeler. He was also responsible for the checkpoint.

"Is this the checkpoint?"

"Yes, it is."

The Pole offered his team passport for signature. The yodeler signed with a flourish, then offered Wyganowski a paper cup half-full of J&B. Not missing a beat, the weary competitor downed it in a single gulp. "Stay with us," the yodeler enthused, slapping him on the back. He held the bottle up, pointed at the roaring fire, and noted the partying crowd with a sideways nod of his head.

But the Pole—exhausted, filthy, freezing, in last place—demurred. "No thank you. I must be going," he said, jerking a thumb toward his waiting teammates. Whereupon the campfire crowd, half of whom couldn't understand his words but had witnessed the way this competitor chose not to compromise his Raid experience by giving into the temptation of easy living, cheered. It was a moment joyous and wonderful.

As he stepped away from the campfire, I made my way to him quickly and stuck out my hand. "Good luck," I said. "You're doing a great job."

Wyganowski was surprised and touched. "Thank you," he said quietly. Then he turned, went back to his team, and marched off into the night.

"That was a great moment," David said, watching him go. "That's the Spirit of the Raid. That's what this whole race is all about."

I watched from the sidelines as the French team Coflexip canoed the swollen, crystal-clear Rio Manso and rode horseback across the Pampas. When a team known as Intersport stole the lead, Coflexip took it back on the last day. In a move that will go down in Raid lore for its drama, Coflexip cinched their packs down tightly and ran four consecutive hours to catch, and pass, Intersport. The thought of running for four hours on fresh legs is staggering. On legs eight days into the Raid and burdened by a pack it is almost superhuman.

Coflexip's time was eight days, two hours. The remnants of Team Dockers, Jay and Robert (Mike dropped out after the canoeing, citing "bad karma") finished three days later. Almost two-thirds of the teams lost a member or two en route.

Journal:

> In the air. Flying from Buenos Aires to Lima:
>
> Funny. I write this and feel the syntax and stammer of the Raid dictating the meter. I think in French, Spanish, and English, which is second-nature after two weeks of all three languages.
>
> I had a wonderful, thoroughly soul-searching time at the Raid this year. Think about it—teamwork, friendship, camaraderie, hatred, despair, anguish, hope, enthusiasm, fatigue, excitement, adrenaline, want, motivation—the Raid is life.
>
> This has been my best Raid ever. I can go home knowing that I have learned immeasurably about how wonderful life truly is, though failure hangs on my heart like a shroud. Rationally, I am proud of all I have

accomplished, such as getting a team together, training and all that.

On the other hand, I am glad to be airborne and dreaming of tomorrows. I won't put my life on hold like I did for the Raid before, though. I will pick my team based on friendship, and I will have a great adventure.

THAT WAS all denial. For months after my return home I tried to come to grips with my failure. You would think that not finishing an event so grandiose as the Raid is in some way permissible. But that very grandiosity is what makes failure all the more galling. I know I wasn't alone in the depression that accompanies Raid failure. Several acquaintances who've stopped early report that they can think of little else upon returning home. They say they count down the days until the next Raid. It's as if failing an event so dynamically similar to life portends a greater inability to succeed—if you quit the Raid, what's to say you won't follow through at work, as a parent, as a lover? The voice in my head (where did it come from, this anonymous critical parent?) reminded me daily of the failure. There was no excuse—not injury, not team disharmony, nothing—for not completing the Raid's great test.

I came to wonder if I hadn't attempted the Raid for myself, but to make my parents proud, perhaps attempting to atone for those years of rebellion and anger with one magnificent accomplishment.

The despair of the nonfinisher is an awful, humbling pain. I would recreate again and again and again the events of "my" Raid. I found myself talking about it too often. Calene got that look of distraction when I brought it up. David referred to it as "Moby Raid"—said I was obsessed. At first, I longed to go back and make it right, just to shut up the voice. Then I stopped longing and began accepting that I just didn't have what it took to finish the Raid. Some weakness, some unfinished wiring in my brain, wouldn't let me see it through.

Then in July, eight months after my helicopter ride, I covered a tall ships race across the Mediterranean. The Polish Merchant Marine training vessel *Dar Mlodziesy* was sailing from Genoa to Majorca as part of the Cutty Sark Tall Ships Races. I was covering five very normal Americans who had won a contest to serve as crewhands on the *Dar*. David was my photographer. Just like the contest winners, we were given the run of the ship.

The *Dar*, I found as I explored her decks during our time in Genoa, is utilitarian in an Eastern European way. She measures a hundred meters long, with room for over 200 crew and Polish merchant marine cadets. My room was a small cabin one level below the deck. The crew slept ten to a room in stifling sweatboxes.

The *Dar*'s steel hull is painted drab Baltic white. Quayside, berthed adjacent to the mahogany and black lacquer *Amerigo Vespucci*, whose sailors dance the "Macarena" at the hint of a downbeat and eat fresh pasta for dinner, the *Dar* looked positively dowdy. But knowing sailors tend to look at the *Dar* with a gleam in their eyes. More than one told me she is perhaps the finest tall ship in the world, able to sail close to the wind, blessed of masts that tickle low clouds, and tapered yards reaching to the horizon like a mother's loving arms. Under sail, *Amerigo* plods as if someone forgot to weigh anchor. The *Dar* hums, a greyhound. I wandered the wooden decks in a daze, ducking to avoid ropes and low doors, wondering if the answers I sought could be answered by healthy blasts of salt spray.

The Poles taught us to climb the rigging, clear to the top of the masts. It is a bucking, swaying sensation similar to holding onto a telephone pole in a gale. No wonder the modern tall ships sailor wears the harness and carabiners of a mountain climber.

And they taught us to shinny to the end of the bowsprit (the pointy pole at the front of the vessel), a sublime feeling that should be experienced at least once in this lifetime by every person on the planet. If I were king of something, I would make it mandatory. Fifty feet above the water, the entire ship behind you, riding the bowsprit—or the "Big Dog," as we came to call it—is akin to floating above the sea on a magic carpet. True, one misstep means a tumble into the sea and at least thirty minutes treading water while the captain turns the tub around—if you're lucky enough to be spotted falling overboard. But that's a small price to pay for a ride Disneyland will never duplicate or surpass.

In those moments atop bowsprit and rigging, a sensual envelopment passed over me. The sea was everywhere, a fluid monster, and fascinating. It changed all aboard. Thoughtful conversation doesn't come easily on land, but happened spontaneously out there. It slipped in when we lingered at the rail an extra hour to watch the sunset. Or when I stayed up late because I couldn't take my eyes off the Milky Way as it split the sky from east to west like the opening to a womb leading to another universe.

Career focus and financial woes and creative happiness found their appropriate order at the bottom of the relevance meter. All of life became larger and grander than anything I'd ever imagined, just like the sea. This is a wonderful place, I told myself and others as I breathed in wonder after wonder. They all said the same thing. A wonderful, wonderful place.

And just when I thought sea and heavens couldn't get any more stunning, a new variable made the spectacle sing: wind. On the third day of our voyage I was high in the rigging. The *Dar* lurched suddenly. The captain yelled up from the bridge to get down immediately. As I scrambled down the rope ladder, the Polish crew hastened into an all-hands position. Then I felt it against my cheek, the gentle nudge of a perfunctory gust. Then another. And another. Soon, the wind was steady and strong and the crew was hoisting the sails—every one of them—and the diesel engine was mute and we were sailing—oh joyous sailing!—atop a suddenly choppy sea and it was wonderful and natural and inspiring and all I wanted to do was stand by the rail to absorb the moment and look down and watch the hull split the waters in the predatory, rapacious way it was designed to.

I did.

This is what I saw: a lone dolphin racing alongside the bow. His back gleamed pale silver in the fading sunlight of early evening. The ship went faster. So did he. I was entranced at th effortlessness of it all.

Then he got bored. Without warning, the dolphin cranked a seamless ninety-degree turn toward Corsica. Gone. Just like that. I searched the sea for a sign that the magnificent, driven dolphin would return, but he never did.

That night the crew stayed up very late. We'd planned on sleeping on deck, but the excitement of the wind made sleep impossible. At 3:30 AM, three of us—I, Don from PepsiCo, and Chris from Columbus, Ohio, carefully maneuvered out to the end of the Big Dog. The air was warm. The wind was holding strong, making the sails puffed and full, the quintessential seascape. The Big Dipper dangled low over the

Med, demanding to be admired. Its stars were like no stars I had ever seen—fat and gooey miniature suns instead of distant pinpricks—and I knew for the first time why ancient mariners searched the nighttime sky with fascination, divining the shapes of bears and rams and warriors. Divining big and little dippers.

And in that moment—moments, we stayed out there the better part of an hour—all the restlessness and lack of career focus evaporated. I was a humble, insignificant man. A dot atop a heaving confluence of wind and star and sails and sea. And more fulfilled and in tune than at any moment in my whole life.

By the time we arrived in Palma de Majorca, my urge to finish the Raid as a validation of who and what I am had disappeared. That moment of serendipity at the end of the Big Dog gave me perspective. I would sail again tomorrow for moments like those. Moments when life makes sense, and we find perspective. Moments atop the Big Dog, between the stars and waves, touching serendipity, and wishing I could write well about it, but knowing that simple words will never match the sensual experience. More than one finisher had described completing the Raid in very similar terms.

CHAPTER 11

Eco Prosperity

Deep in a primeval forest in British Columbia, on a mountainside canted much closer to vertical than horizontal, Team Spooky Bear's Trish Lee collapsed to the earth and swore like a sailor.

SHE THOUGHT she'd been paying attention. She thought she'd taken all the right precautions. She thought she'd found cover when her teammates screamed warnings ("rock, rock, rock") about yet another rain of granite dislodged by opposing Eco-Challenge squads traversing the ridgeline above. But she hadn't. Two rocks the size of fists had slammed into her head. All she could do was lie moaning as her blood mixed with the black soil.

Lee's four teammates—Jim Garfield, Don Baker, Erik McLaughlin, and Dan O'Shea—were faced with two immediate realizations. First, their Eco-Challenge was over. Event rules state that unless all five members finish, the whole team is disqualified. Second, and more pressing, was getting Lee medical assistance. Spooky Bear was at least ten miles from civilization. They had no radio. There was no way to signal a helicopter, let alone find a place for one to land in the suffocatingly dense forest. As Lee began to shiver in the warm mountain air, a symptom of shock, the Spookies came to a third realization, one that hit them hardest of all: There would be no medical care from the outside. If Lee was to live, it was up to them.

Unwittingly, the men of Spooky Bear were proving Mark Burnett's favorite, surprisingly insightful, philosophy. "People think this race is about physical fitness or technical expertise, but it's not. The Eco-Challenge is really about group dynamics, about people learning to work together under very difficult circumstances."

It's about maintaining unity while wet, miserable (because you don't know exactly where you are and in your heart of hearts fear the true location to be that unsettling netherworld between hopelessly lost and you-are-here), filthy, hungry, exhausted (from sleeping just two hours, and even worrying about the extravagance, as truly driven teams do not sleep at all), and standing over a favorite teammate who's suffering from a skull beating too savage for even Mike Tyson to inflict. In fact, at that very moment, if it were possible to determine which of the seventy-five teams spread out over twenty miles in the Pemberton Valley was receiving the best value for their $10,000 entry fee and six months of mind-and-body training, the award most definitely would have gone to Spooky Bear.

Utah, for Burnett, Terkelsen, and Eco, was a coming-out party, a chance to show all of America the epic sweep of racing through wilderness. MTV and NBC devoted large chunks of air time to the event. But that was just a warm-up. British Columbia was the next step in Burnett and Terkelsen's master plan, an upping of the ante to show both competitors and viewers just how tough their race could be. MTV was replaced by the Discovery Channel, which not only bought a chunk of the race and became title sponsor, but sent a whopping fourteen camera crews to B.C. Their plan was to air a ten-hour documentary about Eco over several nights of broadcasting. The similarity to a miniseries was intentional: with all the drama and scope a major adventure race offers, how better to display the action?

Such a realization will someday be viewed as a milestone in adventure racing. As a print journalist I like to humor myself and believe written descriptions of adventure and humanity are enough to do justice to Eco and the Raid. But in truth, the constant struggle of adventure racing makes it the ultimate televised sports event. Soap opera drama against the life-and-death backdrop of mountain majesty can't be beat. Which is why Discovery Channel had fourteen camera crews in B.C. They were the 800-pound gorilla, given to shooing journos and photographers from the action if it interfered with their shot—even in the middle of an interview. Sure, they were a nuisance. And I still don't think video will ever slip beneath a competitor's skin and into his soul like the written word. But for Burnett, seeking to advance adventure racing by advancing his race, the move made sense. "Someday," he whispered to me, "we may not even need all these teams. Their entry fees aren't where we get the bulk of our money. We'll just make it an invitational event and bring only the top teams in the world. It'll be better television."

Again, from a pragmatic point of view, he was right. Realistically, adventure racing may do what marathon running and mountain biking and triathlon did before it, arcing upward for ten years and then slowly fading as some other new, tougher sport comes on. As an entrepreneur, Burnett is bound by nature to shake the money tree as long as he can, strike while the sport's hot. Should it descend slowly and inexorably into that oblivion reserved for marathon dance contests and cross-nation running events (both popular in the 1920s), adventure racing will be a useless entrepreneurial tool.

That's not good nor bad, that's just fact. Just as it's fact that Burnett and Terkelsen were making their five-year plan come true in a big way by the time Eco landed at B.C.'s Whistler Resort. The schools and product merchandising Terkelsen predicted in 1993 were reality (the Eco-Challenge Adventure School was begun in Malibu in summer 1995; shoes and packs were pouring out of Hi-Tec and JanSport even before the inaugural Eco). Where once Burnett could be counted on to show up for any social occasion in the same tweed suit, he moved about the prerace cocktail party at the base of Whistler Mountain in new designer garb. Terkelsen, as always, stayed in the shadows, but the former investment banker appeared no less nattily dressed. Both men were far calmer than I'd ever seen them, a condition that lasted through all of Eco '96. It was the calm of success. The calm that comes when you needn't scramble and be in-your-face aggressive to get people's attention, a sponsor list as long as both their arms combined, and a monstrous new cash infusion from Discovery Channel—it was the calm of money. Terkelsen and Burnett wore success, like their new clothes, well.

Inevitably, others had begun using Eco and the Raid to further themselves. Steines had been the first, using his adventure racing background to leap into the big time with *Entertainment Tonight*. He'd also appeared in a few television movies and had a small role in Oliver Stone's *Nixon*.

The next group included the members of the women's team from

Borneo. Despite their last-place finish, Americans were understandably enthralled with the ladies' adventures, especially when Steines made them the subject of his Borneo documentary. Sarah O'Dell, the former model turned adventure gal, revived her modeling career. Cathy Sassin-Smith raced in every major adventure race between Borneo and British Columbia, becoming so recognized for her successes that Hi-Tec hired her to design a line of adventure racing shoes. Of all the women, she had proved herself the most resilient, just as she did at that challenge of May 1994.

No single male adventure racer ruled dominant, so Jimmy Garfield (American Pride alternate in 1992, Team Dockers alternate in 1995, Eco finisher in 1995 with his own Team Spooky Bear) marketed himself in a different way. Instead of bragging to sponsors about victories, he simple showed them the numerous magazines and television programs in which his youthful, handsome, and persistent face showed up. Wherever there was a camera there was sure to be Jimmy Garfield. All the better was the fact that Jimmy had a great personality and genuinely loved adventure racing. The man who didn't know how to change a flat tire on his mountain bike before the first Eco had blossomed into a self-contained adventurer with the skills and stamina and equipment to race anywhere at anytime.

So savvy was Jimmy with sponsors that his one-room apartment resembled an outdoor gear store. Major companies like DuPont and Adidas paid him thousands of dollars to wear their products and make sure they found their way into magazines. Garfield usually made that happen. So Jimmy Garfield became the first individual in the history of adventure racing to make his living solely from the sport. Far from hand to mouth, Jimmy drove a sports car and hobnobbed with movie stars. In the history of sports marketing, perhaps no individual has ever been as unique as Garfield. Instead of making his name by being a champion, his was earned by being Everyman. In most sports that wouldn't work. But in adventure racing, where even the most heroic acts of the most physically talented competitors are subjugated to the abilities and mishaps of teammates (the "you're only as good as your slowest man" axiom), Garfield's identity was fittingly emblematic of the sport.

Another unlikely individual to find a niche in adventure racing was

Don Baker. Cast aside by Team American Pride in 1993 and 1994 (he was alternate both years) and Team Dockers, Baker entered the arena with his one-day Adidas Triple Bypass adventure race. While setting the course in the desert mountains outside San Diego, Baker discovered that his previous lives as Navy SEAL and San Diego SWAT officer had instilled a deep awareness of logistics. Not only did the Triple Bypass go off flawlessly that first year, but his format (run-swim-paddle-mystery events) was copied by the folks at Hi-Tec when they stepped away from Burnett in 1996 and started their own one-day race with promoter Michael Epstein. It soon blossomed into a major affair, with upward of 150 teams. Epstein, a marketing pro on a par with Burnett, took just one year to turn his eight-city series into the world's biggest. When Epstein's series culminated in a U.S. championship in November 1997, Jimmy Garfield captained the winning team.

Baker's second Triple Bypass in 1996 was also a success. This attracted the attention of the International Management Group, the world's largest sports marketing corporation. Baker was signed as a client, to produce races for the growing worldwide need for adventure races. He subsequently produced the ESPN Xtreme Games adventure race in 1997, the first-ever Chinese adventure race in 1997 (the Mild Seven Outdoor Quest), and another Triple Bypass. At this writing, he is the hottest course layout guru in the world, regularly jetting off to design courses in the most obscure locales. An appropriate measure of success for a deserving individual.

But for all the talk of careers and money, a very real part of everyone associated with adventure racing questions exactly how it feels to compete. Once that addictive sensation is enjoyed, the thought of going back and doing it again knocks at the brain. Which was why Burnett was still talking of competing again, despite his successes. And why Garfield and Sassin-Smith keep going back. And for Baker, the man who had everything but a finisher's trophy, the desire to compete grew stronger with every post-race war story about joy and suffering he heard, but that he was not a part of.

Garfield asked Baker to join Spooky Bear in B.C. Baker had the stamina and know-how, but that was no reason to think it would be any easier for him to finish. Instead of navigating arid desert like in

Utah, which was as simple as setting a line toward the horizon and trekking toward it, Burnett would send teams straight up and down forest-shrouded mountain after forest-shrouded mountain. Endless, repetitious, spirit-breaking. Except for summits above the tree line, tightly interwoven pines would obscure not just horizon, but the sun itself.

Waist-level, competitors would confront a nefarious plant known as The Devil's Club. The top of the Club's leaves are smooth and fern-like. Bottoms and stems are coated with needle-like thorns that grab onto exposed skin. A person's first instinct when stumbling is to reach out for support. In the forests of B.C., the only thing they would grab would be a handful of Devil's Club. "The worst," Team Captain Garfield lamented later. It was Day One of the race. His clothes were already filthy from bushwhacking. His smile was strained. Rows of stickers were obvious beneath the first layer of skin on both hands. "I'll be picking these out for months."

In the valleys, teams would ford raging rivers and be on the lookout for both grizzlies and black bears. "You can tell if you're in grizzly territory by the scat," competitors would be warned the night before the start. "If you're looking at black bear scat you'll see pieces of berries. If you're looking at grizzly scat you'll see chunks of bone."

Because of a bad team experience at the Utah Eco, Garfield chose wisely when selecting Spooky Bear ("Spooky Bear" comes from his association with writer and director John Milius. Milius also owns Bear surfwear, a brand name he thought up for the film *Big Wednesday*. No one's quite sure where the "spooky" part came from). He picked a team he felt he was sure to get along with. Dan O'Shea, a Naval Academy grad and SEAL lieutenant, was selected for overall grit and map-reading skills. Baker, in addition to being a former SEAL and San Diego SWAT policeman, was also an accomplished kayaker. He competed in the 1992 Olympic Trials.

Lee, a lawyer by trade, was a veteran outdoorsperson and—somewhat incongruously—Ultimate Frisbee World Champion. And twenty-two-year-old Erik McLaughlin, he of the pierced tongue and hair dyed white, was brought on board for his mountain biking skills. Somewhat ominously, McLaughlin had competed in three major adventure races—Eco, the Extreme Games, and New Zealand's Southern Traverse—and never finished once. His goal in British Columbia? To finish. Nothing more.

The first leg would be a twenty-two-mile ride and run, meaning that each team would be given just two horses. While two people rode, the other three ran alongside. When runners got tired, they recovered by riding. From there it was on to thirty-five miles of mountaineering, eighty miles of paddling, and fifty miles on the mountain bike. There would be a transition area between each stage where teams could drop off gear from one leg, resupply, then push on. It would be the only time they would be allowed outside assistance.

The race began August 23 at dawn, in a meadow along the Lillooet River. Like a scene from a Japanese watercolor, wisps of fog floated low to the ground and spun into trees, muting and soothing 600 nervous horses and their even more-nervous riders. Garfield, in the moments before the gun went off, went from team member to team member, calmly reminding them why they were there. "The goal is to finish," he mumbled like a mantra, "the goal is to finish." In other words, we're normal folks trying to get through this best we can. Let teams like Reebok and Hi-Tec, which featured the world's best adventure racers, go ahead. Forget them. Stay within yourselves. If nothing else, know the satisfaction of seeing this through to the end.

Garfield had done just that in Utah. When two members of his team dropped out after suffering severe hypothermia, the remaining three marched across the desert in lock step, repeating their mantra. "We're here to kick ass and chew bubble gum. And right now, we're all out of bubble gum." They finished.

Other than Dan suffering the painful indignity of a horse's stepping on his ankle, and the team rapidly tiring of Erik's clicking his tongue jewelry against the back of his teeth, the ride and run went magnificently. When it came time to leave the horses at a vet station and swim the raging Lillooet, they faced being swept downstream and forced to hike back along the bank.

At river's edge was another team facing the same predicament, Team Fit for Life, which included the seventy-year-old Vic Stroud and his forty-one-year-old son, Michael. They'd run through the heat and dust with few problems. Per instruction, they turned in their mounts at the twenty-one-mile-mark vet check, and prepared to run into the mountainous forests of B.C.

But first they had to swim the Lillooet.

The Lillooet is a seething, glacier-fed torrent, a cobalt blue body of water that people venture into only accidentally. Like when they lose their footing wading in the shallows or the bank gives way. Current and cold snatch them away. If, somehow, they manage to struggle back to shore, they become the subject of much tsk-tsk'ing about carelessness and the need for life jackets and being more respectful of nature's unpredictable majesty.

But nobody leaps into the Lillooet on purpose, especially not during August, when the glaciers that feed it are melting abnormally fast, raising the water level as much as three feet in one afternoon.

Lemming-like, though, Eco-Challenge team after Eco-Challenge team appeared on the west bank weighted down by backpacks, gave the river a "here goes nothing" look, and leapt in. The strongest swimmers were swept downstream only fifty yards or so before finding the eddy that signified safety. Lesser swimmers bobbed for hundreds of yards. Weaker swimmers struggled that much longer, and had to be fished out by safety teams on the bank.

And then there was Vic Stroud.

Vic Stroud was in trouble immediately after wading into the Lillooet. The water grabbed hold of him like a claw and swatted him downstream. Safety crews threw rescue lines, but one after another, they missed. Helplessly, Vic fought the current, straining to grab hold of a rope. But the cold water made his movements sluggish, and all he could do was flail. With the river dragging him farther and farther away from the safety crews, Vic Stroud was running out of people to save him.

Michael, already safely across, took matters into his own hands. He grabbed a rope. Ran down the bank. Threw the only throw in his whole entire life that really mattered. And felt the tug on the end when his dad grabbed ahold. Michael Stroud pulled Vic to safety, and wrapped his loving arms around him just to make sure he was really OK. Then Team Fit for Life shouldered their packs and ran on, stumbling into the woods in the direction of the Boomerang Glacier. Drama behind them, there was still a race to be run. Regrettably, Fit For Life were done in by the harsh forest terrain and pulled out two days later.

The Spookies linked arms and forded the torrent together. A half-mile later they were in the first transition area, changing out of wet gear and strapping on the sixty-pound packs they would carry through the mountains ahead. "I'll tell you," Baker confided to team doctor Billy Trolan, "I feel great. I feel like I'm totally within my element." Trolan, a longtime friend, wrapped Baker in a hug.

"Do it, man. Do it. No matter what, don't quit."

Baker looked at him like he was crazy. "Never." On three different occasions from 1993 to 1995 he was selected to compete as a member of the US team at the Raid Gauloises. All three times his easygoing take on life was misjudged by foolish teammates as apathy, and he was replaced. They told him he lacked intensity. To finally be competing in a similar event meant the world to Baker.

Four hours behind Reebok and a French squad known as Life Extension, Spooky Bear trekked into the mountains for the first time. What they saw blew their minds. "It was unbelievably thick forest," O'Shea marveled later. "Thicker than any forest you can imagine." O'Shea marched in front, clearing the path. The vegetation was so thick that it took almost an hour of work to travel a mere half-mile.

"There was this tree called slide alder," Baker explains. "After an avalanche wipes out all the pine trees in an area, slide alder grows out of the side of the mountain at a forty-five-degree angle. If you're not tripping over the roots, you're climbing over trunks of trees wiped out in the avalanche." They slept that night next to a cliff, bodies roped to trees.

Lee's beaning came on the second day. Garfield got to her first, but it was Baker who had the emergency medical training. He rolled her over. There were two cuts, one on the left side of the hairline, bleeding into her eye. The other was centered perfectly atop her head. Three inches long, split almost to the bone.

Baker had to act fast. He cleansed the wounds with a water bottle. So far so good. But how to keep the wounds closed? There were no sutures in the first aid kit.

Baker settled on a McGyver-like solution. He tied together strands of hair from both sides of each wound. The scalp knit together. The flow of blood stopped. Benzoyne, a sticky antiseptic, was poured atop the hair as a de facto glue to hold the knots fast. The final touch, an Adidas doo-rag tied securely atop her head, put Lee back in business. "I trained too hard to let a couple bumps on the head stop me," thirty-two-year-old Lee shrugged later. "I had to go on."

Up and down 3,000-foot peaks. Through rivers. Despite Lee's concussion. The team went on. "It was uncomfortable beauty. The ferns had needles. I'd get my foot jammed in rock crevices. I'd get to the top of a mountain, and think the hard part was behind me," says Garfield. "Then I'd look out at the vista and get totally depressed, because I would realize that we still had so many more miles to walk that it was farther than my eyes could see. After awhile I stopped looking at the scenery when we reached a summit."

Spooky Bear was mired in the middle of the field when they finally emerged from the mountains, but didn't care. They were still going. Over half the teams had quit. In a field that included soldiers, trained mountain guides, and professional triathletes, Spooky Bear—a team of regular folks out to have an above-average experience—were one of the few contestants remaining. They had done the hard part. They ate a meal and swapped filthy, torn team uniforms for new ones. Blisters were bandaged. Trolan sutured Lee's head.

But there were problems. Erik's hacking cough and congestion were diagnosed as early stages of pneumonia. Trolan quietly pulled him aside and gave him the facts: Erik could go on, and put his life at risk, or he could stop. Simple as that. Erik, stunned, was out of another race.

So it was that Spooky Bear began canoeing at 4 PM on Day Three, minus Erik and officially out of the Eco-Challenge. They were allowed to continue without him, but could not be considered contenders anymore.

"This could be the best thing that ever happened to us," Lee pointed out with her usual bent toward the positive. Despite the rocks to the head, she'd earned the respect of the team with her outdoor savvy and inner strength. So when she spoke, the words carried weight. "The pressure's off. Let's have a good time."

"Hey, we paid $10,000 to be here, we might as well make the most of it," Baker added.

For two days and nights they canoed Downton and Carpenter

Lakes ("lakes" being partly an oxymoron, as both were linked by white-water rivers), enjoying the experience all the more because the competitive pressure was off. During sunrises and sunsets, the team pulled over and reveled in the majesty of it all. Mountains behind them now, the beauty was no longer uncomfortable but worth savoring. When a bald eagle or bear was spotted on shore, they stopped to look. No matter that Eco-Internet and a heated group of five other contenders were almost two days ahead, Spooky Bear was having fun. When forced to carry their canoes overland for five miles, the Spookies even made the most of that potentially dreary situation.

"We found ourselves walking through a small town called Gold Ridge," Garfield remembers with a wide grin, "and Gold Ridge had a pub. And the pub, of course, had beer."

The team took a break. Only after two pitchers and fifteen bags of pretzels did they return to the water. "Best paddle of my life," Baker said as the sun slipped behind the tree line.

When the eighty-mile paddle came to an end, the finish line was suddenly tantalizingly close. They pushed on harder than ever. On the bike leg that followed, despite having to bomb down a mountain at night, despite speeds so fast that brakes heated rims to the point of inner tubes actually melting, despite four flats in the fourteen downhill miles, Spooky Bear kept going.

But actually crossing the finish line was not meant to be. The bottom bracket of Lee's bike, that crucial section full of bearings that makes the pedals go round, froze up. The Spookies could either push the bikes the final miles, leave Lee behind, or . . . stick together. The decision was immediate. The Spookies had come too far together. And a quick look at the maps revealed that the town of Creekside was within walking distance.

"And what do you know," Garfield says, "but that town had a bar."

Just fifteen miles from the finish, Spooky Bear's Eco-Challenge came to an end. Instead of hiking to the finish, they set their bikes down in a parking space at the Highland Inn in Creekside, British Columbia, strolled inside just as filthy and sweaty as any group of people has a right to be, and ordered their first pitcher of beer. And that's where race officials found Team Spooky Bear—plus five other teams and a passel of locals—the next morning, reveling in the funky dissonance of the Eco-Challenge.

Spooky Bear's final party in B.C. was the awards ceremony held in the chalet atop Whistler Mountain. In addition to the first-place trophy Mark Burnett gave Team Reebok, and awards to the rest of the top ten, Team Spooky Bear was declared by Burnett to have officially finished the Eco-Challenge. He presented them with the foot-high totem poles specially designed for that honor. And why not? In their own way, Spooky Bear had proved again and again that they knew better than most what adventure racing is all about.

Baker, finally a finisher, was surprised at how easy the accomplishment felt. "Give me a couple weeks to catch up on my sleep and I could go back out and do it again," he beamed.

Garfield made love to his girlfriend during the gondola ride down the mountain from the finish party. "It was a long ride," he shrugged. "I made sure we had the car to ourselves."

Mark Burnett and I have never been more than close business acquaintances over the years. We have even feuded from time to time when my written words about his actions were less than complimentary. But we hugged when saying our good-byes in B.C. "Not finishing in Borneo was the best thing that ever happened to me," he confided, as if the experience had bothered him for some time and he'd finally come to terms with it. "I couldn't possibly have the empathy for competitors that I have now if I hadn't experienced what it was like not to finish."

Borneo seemed so long ago but it wasn't. In the four years since my *Runner's World* story was published an entire sport had taken off around us. Adventure racing was a train speeding out of the station. From just one American competitor in 1990, the sport now listed thousands. From just the one event in the world in 1992, there were now at least two dozen, including the Raid, Eco, the Raiverd in Spain, Raid Corsica, the Hi-Tec Adventure Racing Series, Adidas Triple Bypass, and even the Raid Nesquick in France, for children. One event in France attracted 200 teams! In the US there would be almost a dozen races in 1997. It was exciting to have been along for the entire ride.

As with all things, prosperity brought changes to adventure racing, both in manner of coverage and type of competitor. More and more, television was controlling the way the sport was presented. The races have always been image-driven. Television has always been the best way to tell the story. But there was a time when print journalists and photographers met that need because adventure racing got no television interest. The Eco-Challenge events in Utah and B.C. showed me that adventure racing was changing into a made-for-TV event. Even at the Raid, Marenco Production is the gorilla, with video crews getting first dibs on helicopter flights. Consider: race organizers recoup their costs through sponsorship, not entry fees. So the fewer the number of competitors, the lower the overhead cost. Made-for-TV events don't need fifty teams, or seventy-five, to be profitable, just a dozen of the best.

Also, sponsors' logos are often edited out of magazine photos. On TV, every logo is seen repeatedly. They can't be edited out. Not ethically, at least.

How important is television? In my years of writing about adventure racing I've sold articles to magazines on four continents. From Madagascar, when my stories went to niche publications (those specializing in a particular sport or subject matter, like *Paddler*), through to B.C., when I made more in one story for a national publication than I made from all my Borneo and Madagascar assignments combined, my stories reached a collective readership of substantially fewer than ten million people.

A single ESPN documentary reaches more than that in the first five minutes of air time. When you consider that heavy hitters like ABC, NBC, Discovery Channel, MTV, and ESPN have all devoted program time to adventure racing, it's clear that the role of the print journalist will do nothing but decline. It's almost ceremonial now to have print media on hand. But we're irrelevant unless the news is fast-breaking or television isn't around—and TV is always around at adventure races.

Further, Burnett was even changing his Eco format to play to television. Instead of teams of five, there would be teams of four. No assistance teams. The concept of not allowing teams to go on, even unofficially, after the loss of a member was being bandied about. Word was, unofficial teams made for confusing television. Burnett's actions can't be construed as bad or a detriment to the sport. Instead, they are the actions of a man who knows that stagnation will kill adventure racing. There's talk of a worldwide series of races, much like mountain biking's world cup circuit. The races will be short, three-day affairs. Fusil is planning one of his own. And in America, of all places.

Another change: At the Raid, those going quickly are said to "race." Those going slowly, taking their time and absorbing the experience are "raiding." As TV gets bigger and bigger in the adventure racing world, those who raid will be excluded. And while a part of me thrills at that manner of keen competition, I will miss the Raiders. With them goes the purity of competition for the sake of competition. With them goes a joy, a joy that has made adventure racing somehow separate from the sometimes-crass world of sports, despite the prominent displays of sponsor logos and need for television. Separate because for the Raiders it is still about recreating the travails of explorers so long ago. Separate because for them these races are still about wonder, and I think wonder is a vastly underrated commodity.

As I surveyed the landscape, I began to sense that the arc was complete. When I first began covering adventure races my greatest dream was to break free of the corporate world and remember what it was like to dream big. I wanted to spend more time with my family. I wanted to taste adventure. I wanted to write for a living. All those things had happened. In the greater scheme of things, my blessings extend beyond my wildest dreams as a writer, husband, and father. I'd been lucky to have been a part of something so exciting as the birth of a sport, but maybe it was time to move on to new challenges.

The only problem was that I hadn't seen all the dream come true: I hadn't completed the Raid. Burnett was kind enough to offer me the chance to put together a media team for the B.C. Eco, but the Patagonia experience was so negative that I demurred. The epiphany on the *Dar Mlodziesy* solidified my resolve. I felt secure in my knowledge that I could be happy without ever finishing a Raid Gauloises or Eco-Challenge. Not even watching the heroics of Garfield and Baker and Vic Stroud in B.C. could turn me away from that moment of clarity. I could step away from adventure racing without having finished one. That was certainly no crime.

In February 1997, a friend would describe the Raid as his "passion," dismissing a failure to finish with the knowledge that the passion would bring him back until he did—and then again and again after that. Not for the sake of achievement, but because of wonder and being in the moment and the joy of touching for a very few days the potential we all carry inside, but so few of us ever realize. Only months after he said those words did I realize that the Raid is my passion as well. But I wasn't aware of that while watching Eco. Nor even two months later. I truly meant to answer no when Nelly Fusil called and asked if I'd like a free trip to South Africa to cover the 1997 Raid as a journalist. But I couldn't. I replied that I needed to think about it.

And I did. And I thought some more. And I realized that finishing was important to me. Vitally important. The more I thought, the less able I was to dismiss this drive or shove it into that corner of my brain reserved for frivolous desires. It had come to this: I needed to try again, because I knew I was physically capable. The question was whether I was mentally capable. I needed to know the answer. I talked it over with Calene to get her take. She was wary, having put up with the roller-coaster of emotions accompanying Patagonia. There was no need to tell her how much finishing meant to me, because she knew better than anyone. A friend later told Calene that I was a lucky man to have a wife who let him live out his dreams. "What else would I do?" she answered. "The way these doors have opened for him, he's obviously doing what he was meant to be doing."

"Well," the friend replied, "you could be a bitch."

But she is not. I am married to a remarkable woman who believes in me and my crazy dreams. She understands why I have a map of the world on my office wall and my passport within an arm's reach of my desk (I don't really understand it myself, but she seems perfectly clear on the concept). She understands that I am enigmatic in that I love to travel, but get deeply homesick when I'm gone more than a few days. She understands that one of my greatest dreams will be realized when we are financially able to include her in all my globetrotting. I am a lucky, lucky man whose life has been so very charmed and whose dreams have made a habit of coming true. I owe a great deal of that to Calene. So I sought her advice, just as I had before Madagascar and the beginning of this very wild season of our life. Calene's response was succinct, very much like her original answer about Madagascar: "I'm behind you."

Then I called Nelly back and inquired whether or not an all-journalist team would be competing in South Africa. I want to write a book about adventure racing, I told her, and Patagonia didn't offer the kind of happy ending I had in mind. Would Gerard allow a media team so I could try again?

No. But I could start alone, at the back of the pack, then join any team that lost a member due to injury or fatigue. When Jim Garfield heard what I was up to, he somehow wrangled a magazine assignment in order that he might join me.

And then I am training for two months, up every morning at five to ride and run and lift and write, making sure none of it interferes with family time or work time, like it did before Patagonia. Then I am kissing Calene good-bye on a Monday morning in late January. She tells me to be safe. I will, I say, lying. We laugh, because she knows I'm lying. The laugh has a nervous, "knock on wood" tone—there's no way to be absolutely safe at the Raid.

Calene is seven months pregnant with our third boy. The thought I force from my mind as I kiss her good-bye one more time is that a freak accident will render me the Raid's first casualty, and I will never see my unborn son. Then I step out the door into the pre-dawn blackness, beginning my journey back to the Raid Gauloises.

Three days and several airplanes later I am in the Drakensberg, staring at Gerard over a round white table in the shade as he describes what lies ahead. "Are you sure you want to do this?"

"Positive."

Gerard shakes his head. He smiles, but his mouth is tight. "You," he said, "will suffer."

CHAPTER 12

Lesotho, 1997

As the forty-five-team Raid field lines up for the start atop Monk's Cowl, a tropical plateau in South Africa's Drakensburg region, we steel for the chasm of self-doubt (how will I make it?) through which we will wander in the grueling days ahead. The finish will be the resort town of Port Edward, on the Indian Ocean. For the best teams, like defending champs Ertips and up-and-coming Endeavour USA, that means eight days of racing.

I HAVE no such illusions.

I just want to finish. I'd competed before and been forced out on the fourth day. I'd attached no special significance to my first Raid event beforehand, but the combination of seven months' time allotted in training and then my abrupt early departure had humbled me. Haunted me. And while I tried to set the Raid aside as just another race, I chafed at the quiet inner voice taunting me, telling me I wasn't good enough or strong enough to gut it out, like I needed another attempt to prove I was.

So Jim Garfield and I start together after everyone else. We banter constantly as the first morning passes easily, thrilled to be hiking through mythic Africa. Racing in the heat and humidity, my ambivalence evaporates and I'm completely glad to be in the Raid. Sweat trickles down my face and it feels like progress.

Gerard Fusil and his helicopter—shades of Patagonia—await on the broad green plateau that is CP2. We are six hours into the Raid. Wiping the sweat from his face with a bandanna, Gerard confides that if we are tired of the madness he will gladly give us a lift back to sanity. We smile, Jim and I, strong and confident and deeply in denial about the pain to come. "No thanks," we say, touched that Gerard is worried for us. "We mean to finish."

At the third checkpoint, on the first day, as the course prepares to snake sharply upward along marijuana smugglers' trails from South Africa into mystical Lesotho, Jim and I catch up to a team that is down a member. Lestra Sport has lost a teammate to a separated shoulder. Checkpoint officials suggest in delicate, whispered tones that we adopt Lestra Sport, if only for safe passage through the mountains. We will be an un-Raid-like six, but less likely to get lost.

Truth be told, we don't want to join Lestra Sport, not even for a mile. Jimmy and I have been getting along famously. Foisting ourselves upon strangers feels intrusive. Our packs, we reason with the officials, contain the food (PowerBars, Powergel, beef jerky) and gear (fleece jacket, Gore-Tex jacket, headlamp, compass, dagger, maps, sleeping bag, tent) needed to make it from start to finish. Only when Didier, the man in charge of all checkpoint officials approaches, do we get the word that going on alone is definitely out of the question. "It is for safety," he says, scrunching his shoulders into a Gallic shrug. "And besides, to get the proper feel for the Raid Gauloises, you must experience the team environment. No?"

By then Lestra is already 600 meters up the trail. Walking quickly, we join the tail-end of their single-file shuffle up the steep, six-inch wide path. When they elect to stop for the night rather than risk the perilous trek upward by headlamp, we do too. When they rise well before dawn, eat without speaking, shove sleeping bags and trash alike into their packs, then begin walking at almost the precise instant dawn singes the eastern sky, well, we do too. Conversation is impossible due to the single-file line. Lestra Sport, like any group of people met for the first time, remains an anonymous pack of four.

The subsequent invitation is offhand—"Would you like to come with us to Port Edward?" But in the next ten days, these strangers—François Marik, Bruno Girard, Juliette Oomer, and Eleonore "Leo" de Bizemont—whose professions range from pharmacist to blackjack dealer, will reveal the depth of their personalities bit by bit, and we will reveal ours, so that we become as close as family. Our bond will be shared food, shared sweat, slivers of panic and triumph. When the ending finally comes—the one no team ever wishes for—our family will grieve as one.

I know I am with the right squad when team captain François shares that he, too, hears the voice. He failed to finish the 1993 Raid in Madagascar, quitting on the second day with severe dehydration. Disheartened, he wrote "a hundred pages" in his journal that night. "I have those pages with me now. When I finish this Raid, I will write the last sentence. Then I will throw them in the sea." His words are tinged with hope. There are so many miles between Monk's Cowl and the sea; so many little things that could go wrong.

François is six feet tall and broad shouldered, in his mid-thirties. Pharmacist, former professional soccer player, show rider with twelve years' competitive experience, he makes his living running a cosmetics company. He and his wife live in Paris with their two children, a young boy and girl. There is a strange quality to François, authority mixed with compassion. He's the kind of man who's hard to read—angry or happy, he almost always bears the same bemused expression. His brilliant smile is saved for the unexpected triumph; his withering glare is spent on Leo.

It is his team, he tells me. He's fronted a considerable sum of money to get Lestra Sport to South Africa. But the loss of his good friend Jerome to the separated shoulder on the first day, François confides, has sapped much of his motivation to compete. He still wants to finish. That part is in his blood. But with Lestra Sport out of competitive ranking so early, he tries to fabricate a valid reason for going on. See, though he hears the voice goading him to finish the Raid, François has already crossed the finish line in a major adventure race. "Let me tell you how it feels," he relates during one rest break atop a windy outcropping. François finished the Eco-Challenge in Utah. Ironically, his team, also called Lestra Sport, dueled with Jim's Spooky Bear for the final seventy miles. "First, you get done, and you swear 'never again.' Then you sleep and take a hot shower. You rest, know what I am saying? A day goes by, maybe two. You eat some food and forget what it is like to go without. Two weeks later all the pain is forgotten. What is remembered is the happiness of finishing. Soon you are dreaming of competing again."

"I'll never do that," I tell him. "When I finish I'm done for good."

François raises an eyebrow. "You will see."

Juliette and Leo both have true beauty, though in wildly different ways. Leo is flawless, a brunette with the most perfect skin. Her body is the stuff of fantasy. But while she tries extremely hard to connect with others, there is a self-absorption, a hollowness I attribute to men's worshipping her over a lifetime, that makes the feat impossible. She assumes that any shortcoming can be glossed over with a smile, a gaze, a flirtatious remark. Anywhere else it works. But at the Raid, a place without room for personal veneer, her beauty is diminished by this. Leo is certainly not unlikable. And she's smart. And strong enough to have finished Eco with François. It's just that next to Juliette, who is a saint, Leo looks almost plain.

I first really notice that Juliette is a woman at dusk on the second day. Of course, I already know she is a woman. That much is obvious to anyone catching a glimpse of her narrow Dutch face and golden hair. But her toughness and professionalism make it clear Juliette expects no allowance for gender. During a long downhill hike on the second day—long, as in ten nonstop hours—the pounding causes a relapse of tendinitis in both her knees. Juliette cries as we hike. Not cries as in out-loud wailing, but cries as in discreet, quickly brushed aside tears. Stone silent. "You OK?" I ask. "Maybe we should take a break."

"It is my knees," she says. "But it's not so bad that we should stop." Of course, because it's even worse when we stop. Her knees stiffen. The process of standing again, slipping into her pack, walking those first lock-kneed steps—it's painful to watch. One can only imagine her discomfort.

During the Raid it's possible to help teammates in many ways. You can carry their packs, or at least lighten the load by removing heavy items. You can remind them to eat and drink, because fuel is energy. You can even give drugs to ease pain. But when mere aspirin or even ibuprofen will not do the trick—and it does not with Juliette's aching knees—a teammate can do nothing. Nothing except admire their grit. And soon gender is set aside, because the teammate is neither man nor woman, but simply an athlete. Like you.

So beauty is set aside. But at dusk on the second day, as Juliette changes from the shirt soaked and muddy from paddling and rain into another shirt just like it, only dry, I see her topless. It's hard not to. We're sitting on the same muddy rock. Still, it's an accident that I see her nudity. She's trying to change discreetly. I glimpse a torso lacking in fat. An abdomen rippling with severe definition, disappearing into her racing tights without a roll around the waist. Her biceps and shoulders are sinewy like an acrobat's and I am not surprised later when the official Raid biography shows Juliette to be a former gymnast.

As flawless as Juliette appears, her beauty comes not from her physique, but from the way she moves, and what it reveals about her. A vain woman would have been either less graceful or more showy while stripping. Both are actions drawing attention in their grandiosity. But Juliette slips the shirt off, then a new one on, without affectation. A simple thing. But it speaks of self-acceptance, and will later translate to unconditional acceptance of every team member. I will love Juliette like my sister by the time our Raid Gauloises comes to an end. I will think nothing but warm thoughts forevermore when Juliette's name is mentioned.

The team's navigator is Bruno. How to describe Bruno? He is a handsome man with aquiline features and pursed lips, a Parisian bachelor with the manner of a perfectionist—all details and fine-tuning. He has held the same job as a petroleum broker for fifteen years. When he navigates, the compass is extended at arm's length and the direction we will travel is merely pointed, never stated.

Bruno's words are few, but always specific. Like Juliette, he carries severe pain—in his case, sciatica that immobilized him just two hours before the starting cannon—but is even more capable of stoicism. No tears, no cries for pity. Like François, he is a master helmsman, steering raft and canoe through the biggest water, reading the ripples for signs of submerged rocks. His patience for Leo is also thin, only less noticeable in the silence. Where François and Leo go toe-to-toe, shouting epithets in French and gesturing in anger, Bruno's opinions are his own. Just once, when he feels Leo is feigning sickness, does Bruno use words.

We are hiking. It is dark. Black dark. Leo is going so slowly that the team is forced to stop repeatedly and wait. François says she is dawdling on purpose. "We should carry her pack," Jim suggests. Bruno looks at Jim. A direct gaze, intended only for Jim. "No," says Bruno. It is left for François to scowl and roll his eyes. "Even Bruno thinks she is faking. No matter what you do, do not carry her pack."

And there is Jim. Just turned 33. Clear-eyed, heavily muscled, with a baby face that makes him look just a day out of college. Jim is capable of pressing the flesh like a politician and just as easily able to turn inward during a long day of paddling or hiking. The only time Jim gets tense is when he's afraid or annoyed. Instead of lashing out, he chooses his words very carefully, as if he's afraid of exploding. But mostly Jim is fun. He has an eye for the ladies. He has a capacity to create comfort—his pack is stuffed with feel-good foods like peanuts and instant mashed potatoes. When the Raid turns monotonous, it is Jim the team will turn to for the quick story or joke. Whenever the Raid takes Lestra Sport through a village, Jim is in the habit of finding the one-room trading post and stocking up on more feel-good food—and buying enough for the team. Bruno will take to calling these trading posts "Jimmy stores."

Myself. Husband. Father of two, with another on the way. Writer or journalist or sportswriter; I never know how to describe my profession. Stripped down and raw from my emotional drive to see the Raid through to the finish, to experience the human connection of competing alongside five other humans, to revel in the Spirit of the Raid. I travel light, carrying only mandatory gear. Still, I find space in my small blue pack for personal objects: a pen and notebook, and my passport. A credit card for emergencies. Though my rational mind is fully aware there will be absolutely no place to use a credit card in the wilderness, my irrational mind tells me it's better to be safe than sorry. And a tear-stained letter of encouragement Calene wrote the night before I left, then surreptitiously tucked into my pack so I wouldn't find it until I got to South Africa.

I will read and reread the letter as the race progresses. Calene's belief in my ability to prove the voice wrong is total—more than I feel myself. I'm not wearing my wedding ring as I race, fearful I might lose it. (There is a precedent here: I crashed my bike during a duathlon in the California desert in 1989 and my original wedding ring flew off. It's still out there.) But I have this letter, which I've wrapped in plastic for preservation when the going gets wet. In this way Calene is with me always.

And on one wrist, a thin silver bracelet. My sister, Monique, has just been diagnosed with cancer. As a big brother, so used to making everything right, the only way I know how to help her is by wearing the bracelet through the Raid. When I'm done, I will give it to her as a reminder to persevere.

But I realize the gesture seems hollow, even arrogant, when I reach down and finger the band around my right wrist. Who am I fooling? In truth, it is Monique providing me with strength, for her belief that she will overcome is total and her battle makes mine appear Lilliputian. She is telling me to persevere. Not the other way around.

So there is Lestra Sport. And there are Jim and I. Will we go with them to Port Edward? "If you can put up with us," I tell François when he asks, "we would love to." Jim nods. And we march ever upward into the sky. Through the portal of Champagne Castle, where we drink from the crystal-clear headwaters of the Senqu River.

Into Lesotho.

THE RAID slowly unveils its complexities. The smugglers' trails, for instance, meander along the edges of thousand-foot cliffs. It becomes an act of faith not to look down, trusting that the next footfall will be sure. The trails wind ever upward, through a wind-whipped notch known as Champagne Castle. The former Zulu battlefield with the unlikely name marks the entrance to Lesotho. Alternately known as "The Roof of Africa" and "Kingdom in the Sky" for the mile-high plateau on which it's perched, Lesotho is a roughly circular country entirely within the Republic of South Africa. It has no fences, few phones or paved roads, and nomadic shepherds so accustomed to communicating from one mountainside to another that even when standing before you they yell in an atonal voice. Lesotho is a country I will forever associate with the smell of mint, for it grows wild and common, like dandelions in Nebraska.

But I will remember it most as a land of the elements: raw wind, wild fluctuations in temperature, unchecked rivers. And rain. Unceasing, inescapable, loathesome rain. It began as we descended from Champagne Castle on the second day, then took to the powerful and muddy Senqu River for forty miles of canoeing rapids. The rain chills us and raises the Senqu at once, making the paddle nothing short of harrowing. We overturn four times mid-rapid. "Scary," I write in my journal that evening. "Tension built between Jim and me as we—neither of us possesses outstanding whitewater skills—got overturned time and again. I hope it goes away. I'm a fairly inept paddler and I know Jim blames me for our dunkings."

At no time does getting tossed in get easier. Water flings bodies against half-submerged boulders with bruising force; we are rag dolls in a rinse cycle gone haywire. Gear is soaked thoroughly. Which is fine except that even our special waterproof "dry bags" containing fresh socks and food supplies somehow fill with water. The food we can eat, even soggy. But wet socks cause blisters. And blisters, during a race where you must walk almost 200 miles, are an affliction to be avoided at all costs. "Dry socks are like gold," Juliette, the finely muscled mother of two and blackjack dealer from Cannes, reminds me as she discovers an undrenched pair in the deepest recesses of a dry bag.

Though just thirty-seven, Juliette functions as den mother, motivating herself by motivating us. "We must finish for our children," she earnestly informs me at the start of the third day, then every day thereafter. She force-feeds ibuprofen to Bruno when the painful sciatica bends him double. When François squabbles with Leo, our volatile Air France stewardess descended from royalty, it is Juliette who quietly calms him with a few discreet words of French. She is our soul, given to fantasizing aloud about the wonderful swell of emotions that will accompany crossing the finish line. She always concludes the discourse with a wistful smile and that reminder to make our children proud.

When it doesn't rain, the high-altitude sun comes out for the briefest of periods, but in that time manages to burn forearms and wrists and faces and the backs of necks—anything exposed. The combination of altitude and sunburn makes my hands swell comically, like an allergic reaction. When the rain comes back it brings a chill, leading to fever. For safety reasons we can canoe only from 6 AM until 6 PM (whitewater and darkness are two forces never to be mixed). The upside is a full night's sleep. The downside is that awful feeling on awakening, all brought on by heat, altitude, and the chill of being constantly wet: nausea, elevated heart rate, high fever, swelling in the lips and hands and face. The first thing I do on rising is take four Advil, drink two liters of muddy river water, then suck down two Powergels (a sugary gel containing 130 instant calories. The energy burst is immediate). The Powergels get me moving long enough for the Advil to kick in. Then the constant motion of paddling all day, plus the adrenaline rush of battling whitewater, makes my body forget to be in pain. Only at night, when I stop, does it return. It will be that way each and every day of the Raid.

The rain nearly does us in halfway through the third day. We're canoeing single file, 100 meters apart. We take rapids one at a time. Bruno and Juliette's canoe goes first, to show us the proper line. (There exists in each rapid a path of least resistance; the trick to running rapids is finding it and staying on it. Crashes come from deviation or selecting an altogether improper line.) Then Jim and I. Then the battling François and Leo, who has stopped paddling altogether because she feels sick. Still, François is strong, and they move along quickly.

But suddenly they slow. Exhortations for Leo to paddle do no good. Then François notices how low their inflatable canoe rides in the water (all Raid canoes are heavy-duty, olive-drab inflatables). He yells for us to pull into the bank. We do. When François arrives we haul his damaged boat out. On the bottom, the area providing primary flotation, is a foot-long gash. We have a patch kit, Jim points out, nibbling on jerky. But Bruno only gives him a bemused look, then points skyward. Pointing to the rain. "The boat must be perfectly dry for the glue to work on the patch," François says. "The rain makes this impossible."

But we try. First we rig a shelter of ponchos above the overturned canoe. That collapses. Then we try standing over the canoe, shielding the ran with our bodies. But drops thread their way, splatting triumphantly onto the area around the gash. Our final solution is to fit us all into two canoes, then drag the useless one behind by rope. It works. Though we run lower through rapids, bouncing tailbones off barely submerged rocks, we are making progress. And any progress, even slow progress, keeps us in the Raid. At one point we pass another team on the shore, trying to make a patch kit. We shout to them, wanting to know how we can help. Do you have a patch kit?, we ask. They do. But it's so wet . . . . Their race ended right there, along the banks of the Senqu in the pouring rain. A year's training gone to waste because a patch won't stick. The Raid is horrible like that sometimes.

The last five kilometers of the paddle are the worst, flat water interspersed with rapids far too powerful to navigate. Our shoulders burn from the monotony of paddling and then the labor of lifting the heavy boats to portage over rocks to avoid the unrunnable water. Nobody speaks. We just labor. Then, when the idea of the paddling ever really being over sounds like a cruel hoax, we reach the tall steel bridge at Sekokong and CP7. The checkpoint volunteers have a huge tent set up. They share coffee, ostrich jerky, and thick slabs of yellow cheese with us. The cheese is sliced with a ten-inch commando knife. Not dainty, but highly effective. Within minutes all the ill-humor of the paddling is forgotten and we are prepared to move on again. Yet we stay an hour because it feels good.

Then we hike away from the river, up a paved road then down a muddy trail toward CP8, and the start of the horseback riding. The hike is ten miles long. Darkness falls within the first two miles. The rain stops, then resumes several times en route. The sky is so black as we navigate the muddy road that there is no sky or earth, only blackness, and the hole our individual headlights pierce. The map shows a mighty river, and contour lines indicate we're walking very near the edge of a cliff. But none of it seems real because we can't see it, so fear is nonexistent. Funny. I can hear the river long before and after we cross the wooden bridge. (Was it rickety? Secure?) I can tell by the way the trail switchbacks down to the river then back upward that the incline is dangerously severe. Yet we walk in the darkness without a care. There's a full night of sleep waiting at CP8 (like the canoes, there will be only dawn-to-dusk horseback riding competition). And hot food as we meet Jacky Touzet and Serge Marchand, Lestra Sport's assistance team, for the first time. Jim and I have arranged for our gear bags to be waiting for us, complete with changes of clothing, horseback riding gear, and new food supplies.

So we walk through the night full of expectation. Our lamps bob in the darkness and it feels like progress.

FOUR DAYS in, we begin horseback riding. To protect the animals and give the stage the feel of an expedition, Fusil has mandated that the horses travel no faster than a walk and no more than twelve hours a day. Rather than be upset about traveling slowly, I am secretly thrilled. See, my little secret is that I've ridden a horse just once in my life. I have no clue about saddling a horse or adjusting a bridle, let alone controlling a full-gallop runaway. So I am hesitant as I approach the corral. Leo sees this. I confide my fears. Anxious to show strength after yesterday's weak paddle, the veteran horsewoman saddles a gray gelding for me from the corral. He is strong but thin. When I climb aboard, the gray is skittish. I sing softly to him the most soothing song that comes to mind, the hymn "Amazing Grace." It works. Why am I not surprised when it calms me as much as him?

The Raid competitors are conspicuously colonial during the ride, trotting through the countryside like Europeans of centuries past. The natives who stand along the trail wear little but a wool blanket and, sometimes, rubber boots to keep out the rain. Though well-fed from a diet of corn and beef, they call out for food in the only English word they know. "Sweets," they cry, young and old. "Sweets."

At first it is charming, and we rummage through our packs for food to throw down. But it gets old, like any request repeated a thousand times, and easy to ignore. Besides, we have barely enough food for ourselves.

The most amazing sight is that of three- and four-year-old kids playing near raging rivers or running through knee-high, snake-infested grass. Their homes are miles away and parents are never at hand. Yet the children don't seem to get hurt and are happy, especially when asking for sweets. When we ride through villages and see the parents, they never look worried.

The colonialist thing is lost on us. We don't feel like imperious conquerors. Instead, we feel like cowboys as we make our way across the green hills and prairies, bandannas up to protect us from wind. Hats pulled low to keep out sun, for the rain has stopped. We drink from clear streams, sing Waylon and Willie songs for the first time in our lives, and stare up at a nighttime sky nearly white with stars. When we sleep, it is a refreshing eight hours. The mornings are still bad, with popping pain pills and sucking down water and gel as much a ritual as reading the paper at home. By midday the sun is so strong that I wear heavy Gore-Tex gloves to protect my hands, even though they're way too hot and my hands sweat. And there is a restlessness to traveling at a walk, a futility. My horse, whom I call Pancho, then Bongo, then just Gray before deciding he fits no name whatsoever, likes walking. In fact, he likes it so much that he refuses to trot unless I show him the switch I'm about to smack his flank with. (A look is usually all it takes to make him break into a gallop. The Lesotho horseman Fusil rented my gray from probably dispenses a fair share of abuse.) But in time the walk takes on a beat of its own. I see the country around me, appreciating the green hills and valleys. The distant clouds. The crack of lightning and thunder storms speckling the horizon at exactly 2 PM both days we ride horseback. And though I want to travel faster, I appreciate that I've made it to Days Four and Five. I didn't last that long in Patagonia. The voice recognizes that, too. It turns encouraging, reminds me that I have the strength to see the finish if I can persevere. Just a long hike, a long paddle and a long mountain bike after the horse, and I'm a Raid finisher. Mentally, I start to think about being done, which is dangerous because it blots out the ability to cope with the realities at hand. So I set those thoughts aside and drag myself back to the present, back to the top of my gray as we lumber along.

"This is the Club Med Raid," François laughs, buying a six-pack at a village trading post. The team drinks the warm lager (Lion Lager: The Pride of Africa) that night before a campfire. The horses are nearby, tied to rocks, eating every bush, every blade of grass, they can. Their munching is loud and, except for the occasional burst of thunder or rush of wind, will be the only sound in the night.

There had been a problem at CP8: The bags of gear Jim and I expected to find waiting were not there. Though the Raid organization was very nice, they were also very firm in reminding us that there were 100 journalists at the Raid. All depended on the organization to transport their gear. Still, Jim and I were crushed. No dry socks. No clean clothes. No new food. But Lestra Sport had adopted us already. Serge and Jacky greeted Jim and me with the same kiss on each cheek as the others. And our lack was no problem. Serge and Jacky found new socks for Jim and me. Provided us with food from the pack of Jerome, Lestra's injured member and from Jacky's son. The food was distinctly French, mostly honey and fresh fruit and fish puree (to be boiled at night) but no food takes getting used to when you're hungry.

So as we sip beer and relax and somehow forget about the travails before the horseback and the lost bags (as I dream of my lost supply of dry socks), I can't help but agree. The hard part of the Raid, we acknowledge, is behind.

We are wrong, of course. Club Med ends abruptly when we leave the horses at Sani Pass and strap on our packs for seventy miles of mountaineering. We feel rested and eager. Tent and sleeping bags are left behind in order to lighten our load so that we might travel quickly.

But as we leave, Leo, who has been arguing with François for days, breaks with the team. First she wanders over to another team and strikes up a conversation, ignoring our pleas to hurry. Then, when François bluntly informs her that we are going—now!—and that our pace will be swift, she gives him a weak smile and lets us walk far ahead while she falls in with another team. Her behavior is strange, almost smug. But we ignore her, content that she is safe with another team. In our hearts we want her to drop out, and we push faster. The gesture is cruel, and we realize it. We stop to wait for Leo. But though she sees us waiting in a small hollow beside a cool stream, she treks up a ridgeline with her adopted team. "I think we have seen the last of Leo," François says with a smile and raised eyebrows. He puts the emphasis on the second syllable of her name, making it sound louder and more powerful.

But we haven't seen the last of Eleonore de Bizemont. She does not wish to drop out quietly. Instead, she has placed Lestra Sport's emergency beacon in her pack. (Teams without their beacon, which transmits a rescue signal to a satellite when switched on, are considered a safety risk. Immediate disqualification and removal from the course are the penalties.) When she arrives at the next checkpoint with her new team, Leo pulls the beacon from her pack and shows the checkpoint volunteer. "They left me," she says. "It was a good thing I had this in case I got into trouble."

Hers is a deliberate, malicious act to deprive François and Lestra Sport of the joy of finishing. She will later feign innocence, saying she just wanted to carry her share of the team weight. Though, as François will later scream at her, she hasn't carried any team weight since Day One.

We don't know about the shenanigans with the beacon, so we're overjoyed when Leo chooses to leave us. She's been having trouble with uphill segments since well before Champagne Castle, slowing us considerably by pausing every few steps to rest. Leo said she was sick,

François said she was out of shape, but the end result was that Leo's inability to race hard had become a distraction and a continuous source of tension. I carried her pack during the ten-mile midnight slog to CP8, hoping she would move faster with less weight. Yet she was not able. In fact, to increase her sense of isolation Leo turned off her headlamp as we marched up the muddy trail under an opaque sky. The only way I knew she was back there was by the sound of her hacking cough.

Now, without Leo, we plan to move as quickly as possible. The path is north, to the top of Thabana Ntlenyana, at 11,500 feet the highest point in Southern Africa, then east, out of Lesotho toward the Indian Ocean. Our goal is to complete the stage in two days. But in our joyful haste we turn due east one valley too early and speed-hike an hour before figuring it out. Trying to fix the problem by cutting the tangent between our location and the checkpoint only gets us more turned around. As afternoon turns to a brilliant sunset turns into bitter night, we tramp in circles, searching for the checkpoint. CP15. I'll never forget it. Mountain, valley, mountain, valley, turn around because we must've missed the checkpoint. Do it again. I take a turn navigating, hoping that from somewhere in the recesses of my memory, knowledge of coordinates and azimuths would reemerge. But I can do no better than Bruno, the man who always holds the map, but has no talent whatsoever for navigating after dark.

Finally, too frustrated to coherently attempt further navigation, we stop for the night. The temperature is below freezing. Our feet are soaked from stumbling into streams. A raw wind rakes over us as we lie against the side of a hill, our bodies pressed together, front to back. "I am very sorry," François apologizes, his groin seemingly seared into my backside, "but we must sleep close." There is no question about intimacy, it is a matter of survival.

And in that moment of despondence, simple beauty. François extracts a small tape recorder from his pack as we shiver. Above the screeching wind, we hear his six-year-old daughter reciting a poem in French. I have no idea what she is saying. All I remember is a sweet young voice talking to her daddy so far away. We all shed a tear at the beauty and awkward juxtaposition. Then, wishing we were done but knowing we are just halfway into our adventure, we sleep. Mine is a fitful half-rest punctuated by dreams of warm blankets, heaters, and hot food.

The others fare no better. After just three hours we rise, zip up fleece jackets around chins and noses to cheat the wind, then turn on our head-lamps and wordlessly stalk up the side of the valley again. My feet are soaked and chilled and swollen and beginning to blister badly. I feel all this rather than see it, because I am afraid that if I take off my shoes—they are Nike trail running shoes with the orange swoosh now invisible under a covering of mud and grit—I won't be able to fit them on again. Or maybe I am afraid of knowing the extent of the blistering. Regardless, we hike, going nowhere fast. But our lights bob in the darkness and it feels like progress.

At dawn we come upon a shepherd wrapped in a wool blanket. Un-able to speak Basotho, the language of Lesotho, we communicate our needs to the shepherd by miming helicopters. Where there are heli-copters, we reason, there are checkpoints. The team looks more than a little silly standing before the lone man, spinning our hands above our heads and making eggbeater noises. Which is probably why he grins as if dealing with fools when he yells instructions in our faces.

No matter. CP15 is discovered by dawn. One problem: Leo's new team hadn't gotten lost. They arrived at CP15 during the night. At dawn, Leo excused herself from the Raid by catching the first helicopter out. On the ground, next to the checkpoint's dying campfire, lies our emer-gency beacon, wrapped in plastic. We hadn't even known Leo was carry-ing it. There will be a race jury, we are told, because the penalty for not having a beacon is—we know.

François tries to reign in his temper, but cannot. Even Juliette curses under her breath. For Jim and me, this is merely a setback. In theory, we can always go on with another team. But for Lestra Sport, disqualification could mean they'll be on a plane to Paris by nightfall.

We try to put the frustration aside. We eat a lunch of PowerBars and dried fruit by yet another clear mountain stream. This one tumbles down into South Africa, eventually meeting the Indian Ocean. As, we hope, will we.

THE ALTERNATING misery and joy continue as the race swings back into South Africa. We finish the mountains in less than two days. The last twenty-five mountain miles are a steep downhill through a spring-green valley. We ford a cold river a dozen times, with the trail winding inexplicably from one side to the other. When we encountered rivers on Days One and Two we took our shoes off to keep them dry. Now we don't bother, as our feet are thoroughly thrashed.

The walk is more agonizing with each step, as the blisters on my feet get worse. I say nothing, though. Juliette's knees and Bruno's sciatica make my injury seem trivial. Even François, struggling to accept the possible disqualification of Lestra Sport, is in great emotional turmoil. But no one speaks of their pain, so neither do I. When walking finally becomes unbearable, I move along by jogging very slowly. It's more of a fast hobble, really. But somehow the change in motion eases the discomfort. Also, I gobble ibuprofen. I know it's rotting the lining of my stomach but I don't care.

There is a jury hearing when we arrive at CP23, site of the rafting start. François and Leo appear before three members of the organization, stating their case. Leo is trying her hardest to have us—all of us, as Jim and I have decided that we will continue the Raid only if Lestra Sport is allowed to continue—kicked out of the race. She says we abandoned her. She says she was able to keep up, but there was a conspiracy afoot to leave her behind. Because she was sick, she says, and we were uncaring.

When François speaks he is equally adamant: Leo was detrimental. A nuisance.

Yes, the jury asks, but you still haven't explained why Lestra Sport wasn't in possession of your emergency beacon.

She took it, François shouts, trying to keep a tight lid on his emotions. She deliberately took our emergency beacon and plotted to have us forced from the race.

The jury is cool to all this. One of their members is a Whitbread sailor. He tells François that a good Raid Gauloises team captain, like a good skipper, is responsible for the actions of every team member. If Leo was too slow, she should have been told to stop. As for the emergency beacon, there is no excuse for not knowing where it is at all times.

After some debate, the jury delivers their verdict: Lestra Sport must stop. Leo has won.

François, the composed man who runs companies and played in the rough world of professional soccer, breaks down. He leaves the jury's cavernous tent fighting back tears. This is how he looks when we meet: head hung, mouth tightly drawn, hands over his eyes so no one will see the tears. But we know, because his shoulders are heaving as if a loved one has died.

I go into a rage. Temper doesn't become me, because I say the wrong things. And when I fly into the jury tent and confront them, it's all I can do to make my thoughts connect in a rational manner. This is not right, I tell them. My voice is passionate but not raised. This is a good team. These are good people. Sure, they didn't know about the beacon. And not having it in their possession is very serious. But can't you see this is a deliberate attempt to force them out? Where's your sense of compassion?

It is out of our hands, they shrug. Fusil has the final say. He agrees that a very major rule has been broken. Lestra Sport is out.

I find Fusil in the dinner tent, telling a story at the head of the table. I sit next to him. We smile at each other. Warily. He finishes his story and gives me his complete attention. You know why I'm here, I say. He nods. I give him the same speech I gave the jury. Fusil and I argue. A polite argument, but an argument that strains our friendship nonetheless. He will later say that I should have been a lawyer. But now he talks of irresponsibility and safety. I talk about the Spirit of the Raid and how awful a man feels when he's forced out. Finishing the Raid, I tell him, is precious.

Finally, Fusil lets on that François never showed remorse. If François would act the least bit sorry. . . .

An hour later, François is apologizing to Fusil and the jury about his blatant lack of regard for safety regulations. And we are allowed back in—with just one stipulation. Team Lestra Sport must always remain in last place. Always.

François agrees.

The next dawn we wait until every team has left, then begin rafting the Class IV rapids of the Umkomaas River. At 6 PM we locate a shaded sand bar on the left bank, drag the boat out, then build a fire. By dawn we are on the river again. At Riverside we leave the rafts and hike a day through jungle to circumvent monstrous Deepdale Falls. We get lost again at dark, but an entire village walks with us until they are sure we are on the right trail. We sleep a few hours on the edge of a swamp, then move again in darkness. We would have slept longer, but a passing team wakes us.

François and I dream aloud of food as we walk through the jungle toward Hella Hella Gorge, where we'll board rafts again. I want black coffee, I say. Just black coffee—and maybe the newspaper.

François laughs. That is all? I would like eggs and sausage and muffins, he says. I would like jam and coffee and a bathroom with running water.

Then we both laugh, because these thoughts are so absurd. Because the soles of our feet hurt terribly, and laughter can be like medicine sometimes. Because the only sustenance in our packs is honey and liters of muddy water.

Then, a miracle. On the far side of the Hella Hella Bridge we come across a hunting lodge. This is the checkpoint. It is a sprawling white house with manicured lawns and colorful fenced flower gardens. Best of all, breakfast is being served on the terrace. Everything François and I dreamed of lies before us: platters of fried eggs, sausage, hot bran muffins, orange juice, clean water. Coffee. Lestra Sport sits down. Jimmy pays the fifty-rand charge. For an hour we linger in this intoxicating mirage.

When we leave, it is eagerly. Refreshed. Back in the boats for a final day of rafting, we can almost touch the finish line. From the end of the rafting it will be "just" (physical challenges have a way of becoming minimized during the Raid) 100 miles of mountain biking, before a final short canoe paddle to Port Edward. It all seems so close, so easy, so free from the prospect of calamity. Morale is soaring. Our stomachs are full. How are we to know the breakdown is just around the corner?

Right about this time, Ertips is crossing the finish line. After eight days, eight hours, and forty-eight minutes, the defending champs stroll under a simple black-and-white banner on the beach at Port Edward. Fusil is there, shaking hands and spraying Champagne. Seventy-one minutes later, Endeavour USA crosses the line. After 450 miles of racing, it's that close. Amazingly, this squad of four New Zealanders and one South African living in Los Angeles (hence, USA) could have been even closer. Coming out of the mountains they were assessed a one-hour penalty for navigating along a road instead of a mandated trail. All that is forgotten as both teams return to civilization and the luxuriant pleasures of hot showers, cold air-conditioning, and sleeping on mattresses instead of the ground.

Back in the Zulu homeland of Kwazulu Natal, the Umkomaas River is running high. Every square inch of our raft is filled with gear as we paddle, legs straddling the pontoons. I'm on the left, up front, as we come around a bend just five minutes after leaving the tranquil bed-and-breakfast. We drop almost immediately into a frothing wall of water and boulders. Bruno is calling instructions from the back, alternating French and English. "Back paddle" and "allez" are soon incomprehensible as the rapid's roar rises to something approximating a fully laden jumbo jet approaching takeoff.

And that's when things go wrong. We paddle hard left to miss a house-sized boulder then drop down a three-foot waterfall. The boat is halfway down the face when gravity folds the back end over the front like a taco. Bruno tumbles on top of me. For a split-second I'm cognizant of how weird it is that Bruno can fall from the back of the boat instead of having to clamber over that mound of gear—how cool, I think—and then I wonder whether the rapid I know I am about to fall into is one of those too-powerful forces that will hold a rafter under for months, keeping the body even as it decomposes, never to be found again.

Then I'm in. Headfirst, though suddenly up and down don't matter. The water isn't cold, but the sudden immersion is shocking. I am no longer in a safe place, but a vicious pummeling spot where the only currency that matters is the ability to breathe—and I have none.

I open my eyes to the surreal sensation of a world of very loud bubbles. Then feel the pain of bouncing from rock to rock like a human pinball. My left knee is dragged along the coarse surface of a boulder, and while I can't see it I know it is bleeding. But mostly there is the fear that I'll never see the surface again. I force myself not to think about it, lest panic paralyze me. What I do is pray.

The rapid spits me out. And everyone is fine. Everyone except Juliette, who was trapped beneath the overturned raft as it bounced from rock to rock. I try to imagine her claustrophobia and panic as she fought for air with several hundred pounds of raft and gear pushing her under. She weeps when we finally push the raft to the bank. She weeps for her children and begs to see them again, slipping into delirium and shock before our eyes. And while she bravely gets back in, Juliette is never the same after our journey through the spin cycle. She is able to do nothing more than sit atop a pontoon and clutch a paddle. Not dip it in the water. Not waggle it back and forth. Just clutch the aluminum paddle like it means life. So she strangles the neck, and she stares straight forward.

Our paddle lasts the rest of the day, until it gets so late that we can't possibly make the checkpoint before sunset. All of us groan— our plans were to start the mountain bike tonight, when it is cool. Waiting until morning to complete the paddle means we will start cycling under the worst possible conditions: blazing, daytime heat.

But the Raid organization comes to our rescue. At 5:30 a helicopter lands on a wide sandbar in the middle of the Umkomaas. A Raid official jumps out and runs to the edge. He yells that we can continue paddling past the 6 PM cutoff. "The end of the rafting is just eight kilometers away," he says. "Don't worry about the darkness. Just keep going."

We are paddling alongside another team now, a group of Parisian college students known as Team 69. Their helmsman is a veteran water man, Canard ("duck" in French). Though the back end of their raft is flat (most rafts have partitioned pontoon sections, so when one section springs a leak the raft can still float despite the deflated section), Canard is still able to maneuver 69 through the biggest rapids. He has simply moved all their team gear and team members to the forward section. Only Canard sits near the back end, his butt hanging out over the whitewater. Yet he never topples from his precarious perch, never even appears worried. In fact, Canard has team 69's crippled raft moving faster than our healthy boat. So we tuck in behind this professional and follow his line through rapid after rapid. His expertise is our safety blanket.

At dusk we pass Zulu women bathing in the shallows of a calm flat section. They hide behind rocks and yell out to us. With smiles on their faces, some swim toward the raft and try to splash us.

Through the day, we've run so many rapids that the process has become routine. Even during big water, Jim and I, who are on the left and right front pontoons, carry on a conversation. Careers, money, life, religion. Sometimes François yells a comment from the back, or Bruno attempts a joke. Paddle, paddle, talk, talk.

But once darkness falls Lestra Sport's concentration returns. No rafter should attempt whitewater in darkness. One slip and we're in and under. For a team to find an injured member in the dark would be nearly impossible. The chance of another boat coming behind to perform a rescue is nil. So talk is out of the question anymore, even on little rapids that barely rock the boat.

We bore into Canard's line all the more. We are dangerously close, just ten feet behind, but we don't dare lose sight of this master and his magical notions of the safest route through. Every time we come around a bend there is the hope that the lights of the hustle-bustle headquarters will be shining, but bend after bend passes and we see nothing but black, silent riverbank.

Then we lose Canard. All it takes is a moment's lapse and Team 69 is no longer in front of us. The thunder of impending whitewater is all we hear. Bruno clambers to the front and squints into the rapid, seeking to quickly discern which path to follow. "Left," he shrugs. "Or maybe right."

Instead, he takes us straight. Boulders leap out of the darkness on both sides. Jim and I frantically paddle. The boat bobs up and down violently, then spins right. "Back paddle, back paddle," Bruno screams. And we do, but it's too late. The nose of the raft slams into a rock. We ricochet off backward. Jim and I still face forward, but the raft is moving in the other direction. Bruno is now at what could be called the front.

We plunge over a small waterfall backward, then into a hole that launches tongues of chill water up over the sides of the boat, soaking all of us. "I was just dry," I cry out, attempting humor. But there is no response—everyone is too focused on attacking the rapid. And that's what we must do to make it through safely. Attack, attack, attack. JAM the paddles into the unseen water, then draw them back and JAM them in again. The river will control us if it can, and our only defense is to paddle hard—to get the boat moving faster than the water, thereby making for greater maneuverability.

All of Lestra Sport have a vivid memory of flipping over in Hella

Hella Gorge, and the fear and adrenaline surge and momentary confrontation with mortality that ensued. "This is a very dark ride," I think to myself. Then another thought: This is not Disneyland.

Bruno is hoarse from yelling so hard. Looking quickly at Jim, I see wide eyes and a drawn face—Jim's only outward sign of concern. "GO, GO, GO, GO, GO" is all Bruno can say now. And we dig our paddles into the roiling water, trusting implicitly that if we paddle with every ounce of energy in our arms and shoulders and backs and abs, that Bruno will steer us to calm water, where we will enjoy a brief respite before another rapid is sucking us in.

Then we are through. The boats stops heaving like a bronc. A gentle eddy spins us gracefully back into the forward position. And one by one we let out a slow breath, then curse, then say as one, "Where's that assistance point?"

"There."

Juliette lives. She points into the distance. Before us, a half-mile on the right, atop a bluff, a four-wheel drive vehicle is shining its lights on the day's final rapid. High-fives with paddles all around. Smiles. Even from Juliette.

Then Canard is before us again, popping in from the darkness like the Cheshire cat. "Where have you been?" he teases in French.

The last rapid goes quickly. We round the bend by the lights of a Land Rover and enter a world of light and noise. Spotlights mark the assistance point. Otis Redding blasting on a tape deck marks the party going on.

Serge and Jacky meet us at the shore with hugs, a kiss on each cheek, and a liter of coke. While the four male competitors of Lestra Sport walk to the team's campsite, Serge and Jacky assist Juliette to a waiting doctor.

It is 9 PM. A group of six teams already at the assistance point are planning on starting the mountain bike at midnight. We will go with them, François says. The question, however, is if Juliette will be able.

I limp on my blistered feet to where she is stretched out on a sleeping bag. Juliette's eyes are shut, her face is slack. "Juliette," I say softly. "You can do this. We'll help you."

"Oh, I must," she whispers. "I must do it for my children."

AT MIDNIGHT, we switch into mountain bike gear and mount up with a half-dozen other teams. We will travel in a pack. Juliette should quit here, but, despite mumbling incoherently, she does not. We pedal with a single-file line of teams. Bruno and François both wear the blue-and-white Lestra Sport colors. I follow their pace, from thirty yards back. We travel twenty-five quick miles without speaking. I assume Jim and Juliette are right behind me.

But when François stops to refill his water bottles from a creek, I see that it's not François at all. Nor is the other person in blue and white Bruno. Dumbfounded, I sit by the side of the road and wait for Lestra Sport. And wait. Finally, when I can see no teams ahead or behind, I realize with a start that Lestra Sport is far ahead of me. I curse my stupidity and ride as fast as I can to catch up.

St. John's Mission is the site of the next checkpoint. I somehow find the red-brick sanctuary, with its shade-covered courtyard, but Lestra Sport is not there. Not quite sure what to do, I drink a gallon of clear water from the rainwater holding tank, then take a nap in the shade.

A half-hour later I'm being awakened by a member of the organization, a young woman. "You are with team five?" she asks slowly.

"Yes. Where are they?"

"They have abandoned the race. One of their members is very sick. You can either drive with us to the next assistance point, or go on with another team."

I was too shocked to speak. Finishing has been my goal all along, but having come to know Lestra Sport—indeed, having come to revel in their company—finishing without them will feel odd. This is a journey I could not have taken by myself. I search for the answer, truly doubting I have what it takes to push on without Lestra Sport, but knowing I have to try. I've come too far, put too much on hold, not to.

The organization woman is waiting for an answer. My silence—and the inner conflict accompanying it— is clearly making her uncomfortable. On the one hand, I think, Jimmy and I swore to finish or fail with Lestra Sport. If I quit now I can safely go home and say I had no choice, that I was just doing the honorable thing. On the other hand, I came to finish. No amount of explanation or rationalization will dispel the disappointment of a second failure. "Well," I say, trying to look more certain than I feel. "I guess I'll just have to go alone."

After we became separated, Juliette had passed out along the side of the road, a victim of dehydration and fatigue. Raid officials use Juliette's evacuation as an excuse to disqualify all of Lestra Sport, including Jim. François, Bruno, and he are capable of finishing, but will not be allowed to. Juliette's collapse has dropped Lestra Sport so far behind the field that officials fear for their safety. After seeing Juliette put safely aboard a helicopter, the three men pile into a Raid organization van. They will spend the night in the luxury of Port Edward. Only by the luck of getting separated am I allowed to continue. "This is my passion," François tells me later, describing why he was glad I was allowed to go on. "I'll be back to finish some other year. Someday I will finish the Raid Gauloises."

And while he could have, François never admonishes Raid officials about the irony of Juliette's circumstances: When she passed out, and they were sure help was needed immediately, François dug the emergency beacon from his pack and flipped it on to summon assistance by satellite.

The emergency beacon was broken.

And so it is that I find out how much I have come to need Lestra Sport. The near-impossible mountain bike stage (example: the course opens with a seven-mile climb up a twenty-percent grade) has been designed by two-time Tour de France champion Laurent Fignon. In my darker moments I swear the design is an act of arrogance—Fignon's way of showing Raid Gauloises athletes that their race is hardly comparable to his. There's nothing that could make that course feel easy, but it would have been a kinder place alongside Lestra Sport. Without them to motivate me and make stupid jokes and share food, I feel like—and the befuddled locals emerging from their thatched-roof huts look at me like— a solitary Sisyphus halfway around the world from home, pedaling a mountain bike up and down mountain after mountain. My feet throb with every step, the sweat dripping from my body and soaking my clothing dries and causes chafing, and I feel dizzy from low blood sugar and dehydration.

Worst thing is, I'm mentally already at the finish line. We were ten days in when the team abandoned. Close enough that finishing was no longer a matter of "if" but "when." And because of that—because my heart is no longer in the race, but 100 miles distant in Port Edward—I lose the desire to continue. I decide to quit. Not even the silver bracelet or my other motivational technique of resetting my watch to California time can get me out of this mess.

Then the camera crew refuses me a ride. Exhaustion and dehydration and the heat hit me hard, causing that low emotional state endurance athletes refer to as "bonking." It's when the body turns inward as a survival mechanism. Anger becomes the only emotion, taking on a very rational hue. The best thing to do is rest and eat and drink, but it feels a whole lot better to be mad. So, feeling petulant and angry and altogether screwed, I pedal onward. By the time I reach the next checkpoint, where organization personnel finally offer the ride I so desperately wanted, I am better. I turn the ride down.

Raiding alone is hard. Especially when the temperature is 120 degrees and your legs haven't an ounce of energy left. Especially when you've tried taking your mind off the solitude by singing every song you can remember, including all of side four of The River, even the instrumental riffs. Especially when even that doesn't work and the inner voice quietly agrees that maybe going on alone isn't such a good idea.

But I keep going. The sardines and cheese given to me by the passing French video crew actually make the situation more bearable. For company, I ride awhile with a team of French television personalities, TF1, who are very kind and like to smoke the occasional cigarette during rest breaks. I also ride with the all-women Spanish team, Buff. They are kind, too, and good company. But when the mountain bike stage comes to an end in a pasture along the Umtamvuna River, it is time for me to say good-bye. Buff will paddle forty kilometers by canoe to the finish. I will take advantage of an option in the Raid guidebook that allows for mountain biking to the finish instead of canoeing. So as Buff leaves their bikes and changes back into life jackets, I go back to the trail and pedal the last forty kilometers on my own. A soft summer rain falls on my shoulders as I hunch over the bars. There is wind in my face and it feels like progress.

I make it to the Indian Ocean. I walk under the black-and-white Raid Gauloises finish banner on the beach. I find François, Bruno, Jimmy, and a recovering Juliette to swap hugs. I even find that imperious cameraman to thank him for not giving me a ride because it feels so damn good to finish. Then I sit down on the bed in my air-conditioned hotel room, peel off the filthy clothes I've been wearing since Day One, and feel a calming swell of relaxation after twelve days of nonstop activity. I slip off the silver bracelet and slip on my wedding ring. My ring finger is far too swollen for the gold band but I jam it on anyway.

I call Calene. "Hey," I say. "I did it." At least that's what I try to say. I choke on the last words, so happy to finally shake the ghost of failure. My tears are joyful and powerful, not at all like those anguished drops from Patagonia. Indeed, Patagonia seems so long ago. So suddenly meaningless.

I set the phone down gently when we are done. And the inner voice, as I reflect on how sweet life feels after struggle, fades to nothing.

What It Feels Like To Finish the Raid Gauloises

NO TRIP is ever over until I step in the front door. Which is why, having accepted a lucrative two-day assignment to cover a dogsled race on my way home, I found myself in a log cabin deep in the Wyoming backcountry with thirty of the world's best mushers. Outside, it was twenty below. Beards, parkas, body odor, and dog talk pretty much sum up everything I could see or smell or hear.

Forty hours before I'd been poolside at the Wild Coast, a rather swank resort on the Indian Ocean, hanging out with David as Tony flirted with Fanny in the shallow end. All around, women were sunbathing topless. Other than stark juxtaposition, however, the resorts of South Africa have nothing whatsoever to do with dogsled racing, so I won't explain fully what I could see or smell or hear there. All that needs to be said is that five airports, nine time zones, and an unexpected snowmobile ride later, I was hunkered over a cup of much-needed coffee.

Bear in mind, the trip into the backcountry was unexpected. When representatives from the International Stage Stop Sled Dog Race met me at the Jackson airport, all I expected was a ride to my hotel and a bulging press kit. I was still exhausted from the Raid. The combination of time change and a day in the air wasn't making things any better. All I wanted to do was check in, take the longest shower in the history of mankind, and sleep until dawn, which was at least fifteen hours away.

What I got instead from my well-meaning hosts was a full-scale immersion into the dogsled culture. After being fitted for a snowmobile suit, helmet, and gloves, I was driven thirty miles south to a trailhead in Alpine. A caravan of snowmobilers was leaving from there to a snowbound ranch known as the Box Y, where the mushers and teams were spending the night. As I zipped along on my snowmobile at forty-five miles per hour, adjusting to the shock of temperature change (120 above to twenty below), wind blasted up under my face shield, stealing my breath and burning my cheeks. The extreme cold and force of wind conspired to make my face feel like a blowtorch was being applied directly to the first layer of skin. I never fully understood the concept of windburn until that very moment.

So there I was, cold, exhausted, singed, eager to get home to my family after three weeks away, on my way to spend a night in a communal cabin instead of a private hotel room . . . and I couldn't have been happier.

Really, what was there to complain about? Riding into the wilderness on a snowmobile is my job, which, whenever I think about it and contrast it with my years laboring in the corporate world, is a pretty cool thought. The snow was perfect white-white; the almost frozen, sun-dappled Grays River paralleled the trail; and, when we stopped for a break (Kit-Kat chocolate bars for a blast of quick energy), the winter silence was total, calming. My office cubicle never, ever looked that dazzling.

On top of that, I was still buzzing from seeing the Raid through from start to finish. I thought of that parallel between the Raid and life again, deciding that it applied. Making dreams come true at the Raid and in life means perseverance, accepting personal limitations in order to work well within a team, striking out alone if that's what it takes to see a goal through, and being able to live in the moment.

I didn't know those sensations before I entered the world of adventure racing. Having touched them, I never want to shy away. Their embrace makes me feel capable not just of attaining greater dreams, but of being happy whatever my lot.

How does it feel to finish the Raid Gauloises? Sublime and richly satisfying and humbling—the way all great big, fat dreams feel when they come true.

Acknowledgments

IF NOTHING else, adventure racing has taught me the importance of personal limitations and the deep value of friendship. Here's the short list of all those making this book possible.

Matt and Donna Laforet in Atlanta, for the use of their kitchen table while I wrote chapters 3 and 4.

Bob Babbit, for getting me started.

Gerard Fusil, Nelly Fusil-Martin, Didier Cloos, Mark and Diane Burnett, Brian Terkelsen, Michael Epstein, Ted Newland, Dave Hanna, Amby Burfoot.

The writing teachers: Ann Butler and Beth Hagman.

Terry Martin, the man who knows everyone.

Brett Sievert of Performance for the Madagascar gear, Keith Bruce for the Patagonia deal.

Patagonia sponsors: Dockers, North Face, Adidas, PowerBar, Kelty, Glacier Gloves, Troxel, Smith, Aquaseal, La Sportiva, Quintana Roo, Patagonia, Kayak Tahoe, Benik, Sealskinz, Alpine Aire, Empact, Silva, Spyderco, Gerber, Basic Design, Professional Choice, Outdoor Research, Cytomax. A very special thanks to Roland and Margo Hemond.

Lesotho: Allsop Softride, PowerBar, Rock 'n' Road Cyclery of Mission Viejo.

The journos: Sean Arbabi, Aris Mihich, Lars, Adrian the Mad Argentinean, Nathan "OK Guy" Bilow, Luc de Tienda, Antoine le Tenneur, Mark Steines, Jon Markman, Graem Sims, and the very wonderful Pamela Miller. Tony DiZinno, for keeping the bar high. And David Tracey, for laughter and good company on five continents.

The Ragged Mountaineers: Jeff Serena, Katie McGarry, Tom McCarthy, Jon Eaton, and Dan Kirchoff.

Bruce Springsteen, for everything he's ever written. But specifically The River album and "Secret Garden," which kept me sane on Day 11, and "Badlands."

Paul Bermudez and the Cutty Crew for Genoa and the Med. Tom Kiely and Carol Hogan for hurricanes and Hawaii. The people at Coors for the privilege of flying around the world supersonically.

Finally, with emotion:
Team 05: François, Juliette, Bruno, Jimmy G., Jacky, Serge, Jerome, and Leo.
My mom and dad.
The incomparable John Townsend.
Monique, for the Valentine, and Austin.
The Bongo Boys—Devin, Connor, Liam—adventurers all.
And, especially, Calene.